The Family Connection

A Guide to Leading Parent Meetings

Lions-Quest *Skills for Growing*
A joint program of
Lions Clubs International
National Association of Elementary School Principals
National PTA
Quest International

Funding provided in part by generous contributions from

W.K. Kellogg Foundation   •   JCPenney   •   Moore Foundation

Quest International Headquarters
537 Jones Rd.
P.O. Box 566
Granville, OH 43023-0566
U.S.A.
800/446-2700

Lions-Quest Canada
515 Dotzert Court, Unit #7
Waterloo, Ontario
N2L 6A7
CANADA
800/263-2568 (In Ontario)
800/265-2680 (Rest of Canada)

Other Program Offices

Australia
Quest Lifeskills (Australia) Inc.
P.O. Box 640
Bondi Junction
New South Wales 2022
AUSTRALIA

Europe
Lions-Quest Europe
Hundelgemsesteenweg 1
9820 Merelbeke
BELGIUM

New Zealand
Quest International New Zealand Inc.
P.O. Box 10023
Mt. Maunganui, New Zealand
NEW ZEALAND

Nordic Countries
Lions-Quest
Kungstat 27
Box 76
75103 Uppsala, Sweden
SWEDEN

Puerto Rico
Lions-Quest Puerto Rico
Banker's Finance Tower
Oficina 940, Piso 9
654 Ave. Muñoz Rivera
Hato Rey, Puerto Rico 00918
PUERTO RICO

Program Donors

W.K. Kellogg Foundation

The W.K. Kellogg Foundation has a 60-year history of investing in people. A particular interest is applying existing knowledge to the problems facing youth. The Foundation assists a wide range of programs to improve the lives of young people in Michigan, the United States, and in various places throughout the world.

JCPenney

JCPenney is a major national retailer, with department stores in all 50 states and Puerto Rico. The dominant portion of the company's business consists of providing merchandise and services to consumers through stores and catalogs. JCPenney has a commitment to the communities where it operates. Part of this commitment is to the improvement of educational opportunities, primarily elementary education and dropout prevention.

Moore Foundation

The Moore Foundation is a private family foundation that was created in the early 1960s by the late Frank M. Moore. The Foundation encourages educational projects that will help children to become thinking, caring, informed, and responsible citizens. Particular emphasis is placed on improving the quality of teacher education and the prevention of substance abuse.

Supporting Organizations

Building local and national partnerships has always been a cornerstone of Quest International. We believe that cooperation, not competition, will be essential in creating a world that cares deeply for its young people.

It is with the support and cooperation of many like-minded organizations that we are better able to serve young people, their families, and communities worldwide.

American Association of School Administrators

National Council of Juvenile and Family Court Judges

Lions-Quest Program Development

Quest International

Founder and Chairman: Rick Little
Chairman and CEO: Donna M. Alvarado
Divisional Vice President: Joyce Phelps
Vice President of Program Development: Sue Carroll Keister
Director of Elementary Programs: Judy Graves

Senior Editor:	Hank Resnik	Production Assistants:	Kathy Howell
Senior Writers:	Linda Barr		Patricia Walton
	Carole Gerber	Director of Publishing:	LeRoy Wittemire
Writers:	Carol Apacki		
	Dick Kinsley	Art Director:	Victoria Boyle
	Marba Wojcicki	Design Assistant:	Jane Ries
Technical Assistance:	Leslie Ressa	Copy Editor:	Christine Neuzil
	Sandy Spence	Illustrators:	Erin Apacki
Program Assistants:	Lynne Taylor		Ron Lieser
	Deborah Washington		Don Robison
			Sue Scarpitti

Skills for Growing Review Team

Lions-Quest *Skills for Growing* has benefited from the advice, comments, and detailed reviews of numerous experts in a variety of fields. Each person listed reviewed at least one component of the program. Many reviewed all the components.

Lions Clubs International

John Stewart
Manager of the International
Activities and Program
Development Division
Oak Brook, IL

Jeannette Cannon
Manager, Special Research
Oak Brook, IL

**National Association of
Elementary School Principals—
Skills for Growing Advisory
Committee**

Edward Keller
Deputy Executive Director
NAESP
Alexandria, VA

Mary Boehm-Riedlin
Program Specialist
NAESP
Alexandria, VA

Don Briix, Principal
Clara Reynolds Elementary School
Harrah, OK

Chet Delani, Principal
Josiah Haynes School
Sudbury, MA

Kay Douglas, Principal
Pinewood Elementary School
Monticello, MN

John Flora, Principal
Aboite Elementary School
Ft. Wayne, IN

Cynthia Monroe, Principal
Johnson Elementary School
Cedar Rapids, IA

Jim Oglesby, Principal
Parkway Elementary School
Virginia Beach, VA

Sandy Pineda, Principal
Maryland Avenue
Demonstration School
La Mesa, CA

Lynne Wake, Principal
Fairmoor Elementary School
Columbus, OH

Bob Walters, Principal
Mamaroneck Avenue School
White Plains, NY

Sandra Welch, Principal
Augusta Circle Elementary School
Greenville, SC

**National PTA—*Skills for
Growing* Advisory Committee**

Glenna Gundell—Chairman
Piscataway, NJ

Bernice Belt
Greenville, RI

Shirley Cupery
Wilmington, DE

Delores Delaney
Virginia Beach, VA

Grace Foster
Grenada Hills, CA

Review Specialists, Canada

William Moody
Managing Director
Lions-Quest Canada
Mt. Forest, Ontario

Valerie Anderson
Alcohol and Drug Abuse
Consultant
Saskatchewan Education
Regina, Saskatchewan

Burnadette Faasse
Social Worker
Student Services Department
Nepean, Ontario

Joyce MacMartin
Manitoba Ministry of Education
Family Life Consultant
Winnipeg, Manitoba

Anne McLean
Health Education Consultant
Board of Education for the
City of London
London, Ontario

Linda Millar
Education Consultant
Cumberland, Ontario

Sgt. Mike Pellitier
N.C.O. I/C RCMP Drug
Awareness Program
Ottawa, Ontario

Joanne Taylor
Project Manager
Lions-Quest Canada
Mt. Forest, Ontario

Review Specialists, United States

Willard Ahls, Pharmacist
Mayfield Community Hospital
Murry, KY

Mick Barrus
Education Consultant
Meeteetsee, WY

Romina Carrillo
Greenfield Consortium
Cambridge, MA

James Comer, M.D.
Associate Dean
Yale School of Medicine
Yale University Child Study Center
New Haven, CT

Vivian Cross
Education Consultant
Hartford, CT

Bessie Duncan
Supervisor for Gifted and Talented
Education
Detroit, MI

Sally Edmiston
Language Acquisition Consultant
Albany, OR

H. Stephen Glenn
Author and Lecturer
Columbia, SC

Muriel Hamilton-Lee
Associate Research Director
Yale University Child Study Center
New Haven, CT

Margo Hampton
Early Childhood Specialist
Salem, OR

Ann Hanson, Network Director
Michigan Communities in Action
for Drug-free Youth
Birmingham, MI

Susan Haverson, E.S.L. Specialist
Salem, OR

Norris Haynes, Research Director
School Development Program
Yale University Child Study Center
New Haven, CT

Roberto Jimenez, M.D.
Child Psychiatrist
San Antonio, TX

Nancy Johnson
Center for Alternative Resources
Newark, OH

Edward Joyner, Coordinator
School Development Program
Yale University Child Study Center
New Haven, CT

Robert Kinsley, Assistant Editor
The Ohio Review, Ohio University
Athens, OH

Hernan LaFontaine
Superintendent
Hartford Public Schools
Hartford, CT

Nancy Lick
National Council of Family and
Juvenile Court Judges
Reno, NV

Sara Lightfoot
Harvard Graduate School of
Education
Cambridge, MA

Peggy Mann
Drug Prevention Specialist and
Author
New York, NY

Carolina Martinez
Greenfield Consortium
Cambridge, MA

Marcia Massey
Curriculum Specialist
Hartford, CT

Frances Portillo-Denhart
Cross-cultural
Communication Consultant
Portland, OR

Wendy Ritchey
Clinical Psychologist
Walnut Creek, CA

Karen Roth, Director
Educational Leadership Impact
Center
Wayne County Intermediate
School District
Wayne, MI

Don Samuels, Chairman
Alcohol and Drug Abuse Mental
Health Council
Hollywood, FL

Ruth Satterfield
Center for Alternative Resources
Newark, OH

Sue Smith, Principal
Madison Elementary School
Newark, OH

Edgar Whan
Professor Emeritus of English
Ohio University
Athens, OH

Dewitt Williams
Executive Director
Narcotics Education, Inc.
Washington, D.C.

Mary Wilson
Curriculum and Staff
Development Administrator
Hartford Public Schools
Hartford, CT

Table of Contents

A Guide to Leading Parent Meetings

Preface

Congratulations on being part of a special effort on be-half of children. Parents as Partners is one of the most important elements in the Lions-Quest *Skills for Growing* program. It recognizes that parents are their children's first teachers, and it's one of the keys for involving parents and community members.

Maybe you've already attended a *Skills for Growing* workshop and are a member of the team implementing the program. Maybe you're a parent, a teacher, or a community member. Whatever your role, your involvement in Parents as Partners can make an important difference.

This guide will help you as you go through the process of organizing and carrying out parent meetings in connection with *Skills for Growing*. It provides simple, practical suggestions, step-by-step instructions, and scripts you'll find easy to follow. It's based on the experience of schools and communities that have already succeeded in doing what you're about to begin.

We hope you'll find your participation in Parents as Partners personally rewarding. We know it can be tremendously helpful to the children in your school and community. We applaud your efforts and thank you for your commitment to the education and the future of young people.

Your Friends at

Lions Clubs International
National Association of Elementary School Principals
National PTA
Quest International

Introduction

About the Parent Meetings

"Parents who haven't attended parent meetings don't know what they're missing. They're not just teaching about drugs at these meetings but about relationships between teachers, parents, and children. Everyone learns how to stay in touch." —*Mike Mayse, parent, Epperly Heights Elementary School, Del City, Oklahoma*

"We did the same exercises the kids do in class, so we were able to talk about them at home." —*Sandi Tirrell, parent, Cape Cod Academy, Osterville, Massachusetts*

"Parents have been very responsive to the meetings. The guide for the meetings is excellent. We asked different teachers to lead the meetings, and they felt very confident. They didn't have to spend a lot of time preparing." —*Betty Matwichuk, assistant principal, Aldergrove Elementary School, Edmonton, Alberta*

"Now we try to listen more without interrupting. We use more eye contact and take time to ask questions." —*Judy Wynberry, parent, Aboite Elementary School, Fort Wayne, Indiana**

All of these people have been actively involved in the Parents as Partners component of the Lions-Quest *Skills for Growing* program. As their words make clear, all found their participation highly rewarding. At the same time, all contributed to making the program rewarding for children as well.

You are about to have the same kinds of experiences—and help others to have them. Reading this guide and preparing to organize parent meetings is an important beginning.

---

*The examples in this guide are based on the 1988-89 *Skills for Growing* pilot program, which took place in 41 schools throughout Canada and the United States.

Successful parent involvement can generate enthusiasm and excitement that percolate all year long.

—*Learning86*, September 1986

"Use my mind? At home?"

The meetings support parents in their vital role as their children's first teachers.

Through your participation you can help provide parents with ways to stay involved.

The three 90-minute parent meetings described in this guide are a basic element in *Skills for Growing*. The meetings are designed to support parents in their vital role as their children's first teachers. They provide opportunities for parents and community members, as well as educators, to get involved and make an important contribution to the program's success.

Although the parent meetings were developed in conjunction with *Skills for Growing*, organizations in the community may wish to offer the meetings as a separate program. Perhaps you represent such an organization. There's no limit to the creative ways you can involve parents and community members in Parents as Partners. Consider this guide a beginning and a set of suggestions. Let your imagination soar!

About Parents as Partners

As you continue reading this guide, keep in mind that through your participation in the *Skills for Growing* Parents as Partners component, you have a key role to play. Parent involvement is crucial to children's success in school. It's especially relevant for children in the elementary grades because these are the years when parents normally are most involved in their children's education. They're also years when the school can encourage parents to stay involved by providing new and varied opportunities.

Research has found that parent involvement and concern is closely related to the development of positive social skills and healthy behavior in children. An absence of parent involvement is connected with many forms of negative, antisocial behavior, including drug use.

Through your participation in Parents as Partners, you can help provide parents with ways to stay involved. You can be part of an important service both to parents and to children.

The goals of Parents as Partners. The *Skills for Growing* parent component has three major goals:

- To enhance communication among parents, teachers, and other adults who are significant in children's lives
- To strengthen and celebrate families in all their diversity
- To build a network of support for children by linking the resources of the home, the school, and the community

The partnership between schools and parents in *Skills for Growing* is a continuing exchange of information and ideas. On the one hand, the school has an opportunity to inform parents about the program and encourage them to reinforce at home what their children are learning in school. On the other hand, the program provides many opportunities for parents to share their own knowledge, experience, and concerns.

How *Skills for Growing* involves parents. *Skills for Growing* encourages several kinds of parent involvement. Parents can be involved as:

- Organizers and leaders of the parent meetings
- Participants in the meetings
- Helpers in getting the word out to other parents and the community about the importance of parent involvement and the parent meetings in particular
- Members of the Implementation Team, the group that goes through training in order to initiate *Skills for Growing* in the school
- Members of the School Climate Committee
- Guest speakers or helpers in the classroom
- Guides to students carrying out service learning projects at school and in the community

Also keep in mind that parent involvement can occur without parents actually coming to school. If, through *Skills for Growing*, parents spend more time with their children at home talking about what they are learning in school and doing some of the activities in the *Together Times* Student-Family Activity Booklets, this is also im-

The partnership between schools and parents is a continuing exchange of information and ideas.

Four keys to a family's success:
- *Shared decision making by both parents*
- *Respect for the opinions of children*
- *Clear guidelines for behavior*
- *A reasonable system of discipline*

—*PTA Today*, May 1983

The program brings together parents, educators, and members of the community to teach children important life skills within a caring and consistent environment.

portant. Ideally, parents will become actively involved in the parent meetings and other activities as well.

Parent involvement can snowball when word gets around that something new and different is happening for parents. You can be an important part of making that happen.

About Lions-Quest *Skills for Growing*

The program at a glance. Parents as Partners is part of a larger program called Lions-Quest *Skills for Growing*. This comprehensive program for grades K-5 brings together parents, educators, and members of the community to teach children important life skills within a caring and consistent environment. The program teaches skills in four main areas:

- Self-discipline
- Responsibility
- Good judgment
- Getting along with others

A basic aim of the program is to develop a support system for children that involves the home, the school, and the community working together. The program's major goals are to:

- Develop and support a positive learning environment
- Teach social and thinking skills
- Involve parents as partners
- Promote community involvement
- Foster learning through service to others
- Promote a drug-free approach to living
- Develop and support positive peer groups
- Celebrate and respect cultural diversity
- Provide support for educators, parents, and community members

There are five main parts to the program:

Parents can provide a "curriculum of the home" that teaches their children what matters. They do this through their daily conversations, household routines, attention to school matters, and affectionate concern for their children's progress.

—*What Works*, U.S. Department of Education, 1986

Classroom Curriculum. Children may participate in *Skills for Growing* lessons for an entire year at each grade level, K-5. All the lessons offer a variety of ways to teach social and academic skills. The curriculum revolves around five unit themes at each grade level. The units and their main themes for grades K-5 are:

- Unit One: Building a School Community
- Unit Two: Growing as a Group
- Unit Three: Making Positive Decisions
- Unit Four: Growing Up Drug-Free
- Unit Five: Celebrating You and Me

Also included in the Curriculum Guides is a process for planning and carrying out a school or community service project. Service projects help teach children the value of serving others by learning through doing.

Developing and enhancing a positive school climate is a key goal of *Skills for Growing*.

Positive School Climate. Developing and enhancing a positive school climate—making school a place where children and adults want to be—is a key goal of *Skills for Growing*. Toward this end, the program creates a School Climate Committee whose main function is to organize a series of schoolwide events related to the program goals and curriculum themes. These events help to extend the impact of the program beyond the classroom and throughout the school. Parents and community representatives are also encouraged to serve as committee members or volunteers helping to carry out school climate events.

Parents as Partners. This guide describes a major element of the Parents as Partners component, the parent meetings. Other ways of involving parents include activities in the Student-Family Activity Booklets, *Together Times*; parent participation on the School Climate Committee; and parent support and sponsorship for service learning projects.

Community Involvement. The program helps to create a spirit of cooperation that brings the school and community closer together. Community involvement is encouraged through student participation in community service projects and opportunities for members of the community to have direct input into the program.

Training and Follow-up Support. You may have already attended the introductory training workshop provided for the Implementation Team, the people carrying out the program at each school. The training offers an in-depth introduction to the program and experience with innovative teaching techniques and materials. Follow-up support is available through supplements that highlight new ideas from *Skills for Growing* classrooms. You can also get assistance through a toll-free phone line.

Support and Sponsorship

Skills for Growing was developed and is supported by Lions Clubs International, the National Association of Elementary School Principals (NAESP), the National PTA, and Quest International. Major contributors to the program are the W.K. Kellogg Foundation, JCPenney and the Moore Foundation.

Lions Clubs International is the largest service organization in the world, with more than 39,000 Clubs in 166 countries. Lions have provided major funding for the Lions-Quest *Skills for Adolescence* program for the middle grades, in addition to Lions-Quest *Skills for Growing*. For Lions, *Skills for Adolescence* and *Skills for Growing* are important aspects of a long-term commitment to drug education and awareness.

The National Association of Elementary School Principals (NAESP), founded in 1921, is a professional organization serving more than 25,000 elementary and middle school principals and other educators throughout Canada, the United States, and other countries. NAESP continually identifies promising programs and practices in elementary education.

Founded in 1897, the National PTA represents a network of state, regional, council, and local PTAs with 6.6 million members. The mission of the National PTA is three-fold: to support and speak on behalf of children and youth before governmental agencies and other organizations that affect children; to assist parents in developing the skills they need to raise their children; and to encourage parent and public involvement in the public schools.

Quest International, a nonprofit educational organization, was established in 1975 to "help create a world that cares more deeply about its young people." Quest develops and makes available comprehensive, broad-based programs and services that enable young people to gain the self-confidence, good judgment, and social skills they need to cope with the challenges they face in today's world. Quest's three main programs are Lions-Quest *Skills for Growing* (grades K-5), Lions-Quest *Skills for Adolescence* (grades 6-8), and *Skills for Living* (grades 9-12).

How to Use This Guide

This guide was written primarily for the leaders of the *Skills for Growing* parent meetings. It offers five introductory chapters designed to help you prepare for the meetings. For each of the three 90-minute meetings themselves, you'll find detailed, step-by-step instructions and complete scripts.

The description of each meeting includes preparation and materials, specific activities, discussion questions, handouts and overhead masters to be copied and used during the meetings, and evaluation forms. Throughout, the purpose of the guide is to make the process of organizing and conducting the parent meetings simple, straightforward, and enjoyable for everyone involved.

Getting the School and Parents Together

Choosing a Leader

The choice of a leader for your parent meetings will be one key to their success. Initially the parent meetings may be led by one or more people who have gone through the Lions-Quest *Skills for Growing* training. As other people in your school and community complete the training, the pool of potential leaders will expand.

Parent meeting leaders should have the following characteristics:

- Good listening skills
- Sensitivity and tact
- A positive and enthusiastic attitude
- An ability to blend structure and informality
- An ability to put others at ease
- Enthusiasm for and knowledge about the *Skills for Growing* program
- Appreciation for cultural and ethnic diversity
- Credibility with the community

Choose your leaders carefully and make sure that teams of leaders, if you have more than one leader, are comfortable working together.

"I understand you've achieved name recognition in the principal's office."

Setting Up a Planning Group

"We've never tried anything like this before," commented a principal whose school was in its first year of implementing *Skills for Growing*. "It took some extra work, but the response from parents has been fantastic. Parents are really involved now. They have a feeling it's *their* school too." As the people at this school learned, or-

As a group, parents can effect greater change than as individuals. Parents are like snowflakes. Alone, both are beautiful and unique, but powerless. Parents joined with other parents—or snowflakes with other snowflakes—can make a powerful force. A snowstorm can stop 747s on runways.

—*Youth and Drugs: What Parent Groups Can Do to Create Drug Resistant Communities*, PRIDE Canada, 1987

ganizing effective parent meetings will require some extra time and effort of everyone involved. Because of that, it's important to recruit as many people as possible and spread the ownership around. The result: everyone will share the responsibility, and enthusiasm will steadily grow.

Consider asking for help from your PTA, Lions Club, or other local organizations. Since both Lions Clubs and the National PTA are major co-sponsors of *Skills for Growing*, it's especially appropriate to involve members of these organizations. Lions Club and PTA subcommittees to assist with the parent meetings can offer an excellent opportunity for support.

Another valuable resource you may want to involve is nonteaching staff in the school, such as the counselor, nurse, school social worker, or resource teacher. Often these people have flexible schedules that will enable them to contact parents and assist with a variety of other tasks.

In setting up a planning group, consider the following guidelines:

- Establish the group as early as possible in the school year.
- Plan the entire series of parent meetings well in advance. Develop a calendar that takes into account various other events in the school and community, making sure not to conflict with any of them, if possible.
- Consider "piggybacking" on related events—for example, holding the parent meetings in conjunction with back-to-school night, open house, major PTA meetings, and so on.
- Involve as many people as possible and encourage them to volunteer for specific tasks.

Motivating Parents to Attend

Most families today have busy schedules. To motivate parents to attend the *Skills for Growing* parent meetings and get involved in the program, you'll need to offer something special and appealing. Actually getting parents to the meetings will be one of your biggest challenges and may require as much time and effort as the meetings themselves.

Parents are most likely to attend meetings when they:

- Hear about the meetings well in advance so they can schedule around them
- Know their children will be involved (see the next section for specifics on how to do this)
- Receive personalized invitations from their child, a teacher, a principal, or through a parent telephone network
- Have their child-care needs met
- Feel comfortable about going to the meeting—the location is convenient and the purpose of the meeting is clear
- Expect to take part in some of the same activities their children have experienced in the *Skills for Growing* class
- Understand that teachers and the school think their role as a parent is important
- Know that language won't be a barrier
- Feel that cultural differences and diversity will be respected
- Expect to meet other parents with similar experiences to share concerns and ideas
- Anticipate a pleasant experience—food, fellowship, fun
- Believe they will go home with something concrete and useful

As your group meets and begins to develop its plans, keep these considerations in mind. All of them are discussed in the following sections of this guide.

Some parents may have limited time to volunteer or feel they have little to contribute. Others may be afraid they're not wanted or needed at school. You can convince them otherwise.

—*Learning86*, September 1986

Involving Students in the Meetings

A good rule of thumb is that parents are most likely to attend meetings when their children are also included. You can involve students in a variety of ways. For example, students can greet participants and guide them to the meeting room, hand out materials, lead activities from a *Skills for Growing* lesson, or demonstrate or exhibit work they have done in *Skills for Growing* classes. They can do all or a combination of these things.

"Students were an integral part of our meetings," says Dick Finicle, a parent at Brush College Elementary School and the Positive Youth Development Chairman for Lions Club District 36R, in Salem, Oregon. "We had students involved in all three meetings. It helps to get parents interested in the content of the meetings, and it also helps to strengthen the bond between parents and their kids." At Brush College the students performed various skits to demonstrate skills they were learning in the classroom. "They seemed to enjoy getting up in front of all those people," says Mr. Finicle. "I think I got more nervous than they did."

At Fairmoor Elementary School, in Columbus, Ohio, students and parents met together in small groups during the meeting that focused on the prevention of alcohol and drug use. Each group was given cards describing situations involving alcohol and other drugs, and both the students and parents said how they would respond. "I think it was good for the parents to hear what the kids had to say," says Fairmoor PTA president Yolanda O'Connor.

We recommend that you involve students mainly at the beginning of each meeting and then leave some time for the parents to meet by themselves, possibly after the two-minute stretch. Each of the meetings described in this guide contains specific suggestions for involving students. The children will need their own activities, such as a video or cooperative games, for the time they are not in the meeting with the adults.

"Student involvement helps to get parents interested in the content of the meetings, and it also helps to strengthen the bond between parents and their kids."

Scheduling and Location

Scheduling and location are key factors affecting parent involvement. Consider scheduling your meetings in conjunction with other events that involve parents, i.e., PTA meetings, open house, and so on. To make sure you're on target, ask a cross-section of parents to suggest the best time to hold the meetings. You might hold a daytime meeting for parents who work at night. Notes Cindy Monroe, principal of Johnson Elementary School, in Cedar Rapids, Iowa: "We always schedule at least two times for our parent meetings, morning and afternoon or evening. That makes it easier for everyone to come."

Another important factor is to hold the meetings in a place where parents feel comfortable—examples include the school library, the faculty room, a classroom, a community center, a church, a social hall, or a restaurant. In case parents have a conflict and cannot attend a meeting, plan alternatives for involving them, such as handing out a packet of information and videotapes of *Skills for Growing* lessons.

Keep in mind that since each parent meeting draws on information and skills taught in the various units of the *Skills for Growing* curriculum, it's best to schedule the meetings to coincide with the time when those units are taught at your school. In most schools Units One and Two (Meeting One) will be taught between September and November, Units Three and Four (Meeting Two) between December and March, and Unit Five (Meeting Three) between April and the end of the school year.

Making It Easier for Parents to Attend

Parents may not be able to attend meetings even when they want to. A lack of child care or transportation or a concern that no one at the meeting will speak their language can be real obstacles, among others. To encourage the broadest possible parent participation, consider the following ideas that have worked for many *Skills for Growing* schools.

Hold the meetings at convenient times and in places where parents feel comfortable.

> **A pancake breakfast or a spaghetti dinner is a timesaver and welcome treat for busy parents.**

- Provide child care during the meetings. Students in grades four and five can serve as helpers. If you expect younger children who do not speak English, select helpers who can speak their language. As part of the child care, offer snacks and cooperative games or videos.
- Where appropriate, make it clear that interpreters or others who speak the languages most commonly spoken in the community will be helping at the meeting.
- A pancake breakfast or a spaghetti dinner is a timesaver and welcome treat for busy parents. Volunteers, including older students or members of a community organization such as a Lions Club, can help in the preparation.
- Plan to serve refreshments during the meeting or afterward. This will encourage parents to stay and get to know the leaders and each other better. Involve parents and *Skills for Growing* students in planning the refreshments you'll serve. This might be done as a PTA activity.

Getting the Word Out

> **"We think of parent involvement as community involvement."**

Langley Meadows Elementary School, in Langley, British Columbia, makes special efforts to keep parents informed. According to principal Walter Krahn, those efforts have paid off in parent involvement. One important form of outreach at Langley Meadows is a series of morning coffees for parents held at school. About 20 parents are invited each time, and almost all of them manage to attend. The school also publishes a regular newsletter that is widely circulated throughout the school and the community and is even distributed in local shopping centers. "We think of parent involvement as community involvement," says Mr. Krahn. "Public information is a very important priority for the school, and we're really proud of the professional quality of our newsletter."

Clearly, keeping parents informed about both the meetings and the program is another key to involving them. If your planning group can create a sense of excitement about the meetings by publicizing them widely, this will increase the chance that large numbers of parents will attend.

One way to get the word out is to take advantage of things your school is already doing to communicate with parents. For example, publish the dates of the meetings on the general calendar for the school year and on school lunch menus. You could also provide information about the meetings at the school's open house or back to school night. And you could prepare a *Skills for Growing* display in a main hallway.

Try sending home a copy of the program overview on page 61 in this guide, including a list of the parent meetings scheduled for the year. Teachers could also provide parents with copies of the overview when they come for parent-teacher conferences.

At least two weeks before the series of meetings begins, mail home invitation letters, assuming funds for postage are available from the school or the PTA. If the invitations cannot be mailed, send them home with the students. In preparing the invitations keep the following ideas in mind:

- Use the sample letters of invitation included in Meeting One or write your own.
- Include the date, time, and location of the meeting.
- Ask the school principal, a community leader, or someone else in a respected position to co-sign the letter.
- If appropriate, translate the letters into languages other than English.
- Make the letters easy to read and include children's drawings or illustrations.
- Emphasize that parents will be involved in the same kinds of learning experiences as their children in the *Skills for Growing* program.
- Stress that parents will share ideas and discuss areas of concern.
- Emphasize that child care will be provided.
- Have the students write notes on the invitation asking their parents to come to the meeting.
- Ask that parents sign and return the invitation, even if they can't attend. Offer a prize to the classroom with the most parent signatures.

Take advantage of things your school is already doing to communicate with parents.

Emphasize that parents will be involved in the same kinds of learning experiences as their children in the *Skills for Growing* program.

"He's coming home with something new and different than the normal school routine. . . . The sharing of ideas is phenomenal. I wish I could find the words to describe the difference it makes in kids."

—Ron Ivers, parent, Hazelwood Elementary School, Newark, Ohio, quoted in an article about *Skills for Growing* in the *Newark Advocate*, April 27, 1989

If possible, call parents to invite them. Use an existing telephone network to help make the calls, or ask for help in establishing a new network. A personal invitation is always more meaningful than a form letter.

One or two days before the meeting send home a reminder. As a service project, students in grades two through five can make reminder tags for other students to wear home. One side could say "Don't Forget the Meeting!" The date, time, and location could be written on the other side.

Involving the Local News Media

The local news media can be an important ally in getting the word out about parent involvement and sustaining excitement and enthusiasm.

Begin by enlisting a member of your planning group who will be able to communicate effectively about the program with the news media. This person's main tasks will be to interest local reporters who have done family-oriented stories and to provide follow-up information and facts about the parent meetings. Sending out a press release like the sample in Appendix A may also be helpful. Bill Sorrell, principal of Morningside Elementary School, in Elizabethtown, Kentucky, notes that he keeps the local newspaper informed by sending announcements of school meetings and events to the paper's education writer. These notices appear regularly on the paper's education page.

Consider alternatives to newspapers, radio, and TV. Bulletin boards in community centers can be another effective way to get the word out. You may also want to prepare fliers announcing the parent meetings and distribute them in community centers, pediatricians' offices, health clinics, youth centers, and similar places where parents and youth congregate. Radio call-in shows are another way to spread the word.

Planning and Leading Successful Meetings

Your group's responsibilities can be divided into two major phases: before the meeting and during the meeting.

Before the Meeting

Select an Implementation Model
You can select from several models to structure the meetings. These include meetings

- By classroom
- By grade level
- By grade clusters (K-1, 2-3, 4-5)
- For the entire school

Once you've selected an implementation model, decide on the scheduling for the meetings, i.e., as part of an open house or back to school night or in conjunction with another event.

Become Familiar with the Meeting Contents
Read over all the suggested activities, handouts, and charts before the meeting. Omit any that are not appropriate for your particular parent group and make any other modifications that are necessary. Gather the materials you'll need.

Consider the Logistics
Whether you're doing this as a classroom teacher or as a co-leader with others from a grade level, cluster, or building, make certain someone is handling the following logistical issues:

- Make enough copies of the handouts from this guide for each participant. Design your own charts, using the suggested information included with the description of each meeting.

"Remember the good old days when you could just look at the pictures?"

I liked the way you encouraged group participation among the parents and let the audience get involved.

This was very informative, and it's great to know we all have the same goal.

It was wonderful to see a group of teachers and their principal show such warmth, dedication, and cooperative attitudes. You are appreciated!

Please have these sessions earlier in the year so we can grow with the kids. Thanks!

—Anonymous comments written by parents after a *Skills for Growing* parent meeting at Morningside Elementary School, Elizabethtown, Kentucky.

- Ask students to prepare name tags for the participants by drawing a symbol on each set of five tags—for example, a flower, sun, rainbow, or smile face. At the meeting the participants will write in their own names. The symbols can be a help when you need to divide people quickly into small groups. If you're not sure how many people will attend, try to have several sets of tags in reserve.

- Pay attention to how the room is arranged for the meeting. Make sure it's large enough to allow for breaking into small groups.

- Place the chairs in a way that encourages interaction. A circle, horseshoe, or double horseshoe will help everyone see and hear each other. Make sure you'll be able to move around the room during the meeting to spark everyone's participation.

- If the building where you'll meet is large, post signs at key locations in appropriate languages. Have a greeter at the main door to show the way. Ideally, the greeter will speak the language of as many parents as possible and be someone they know, e.g., the principal, a student who received special recognition recently, or a community leader.

During the Meeting

A successful meeting will be lively and will sustain the participants' interest. Consider the following ideas:

Monitor the Pacing and Tone

- Begin and end the meeting on time. Help latecomers feel welcome. Keep the suggested time allotments for each activity clearly in mind, but allow time for interaction and discussion. If an activity takes longer than you expected, shorten another one.

- Vary the pace and activities. If the group seems to tire or lose interest, divide into small groups, take a break, or end the discussion.

- Provide ideas and suggestions the participants can use at home. These might include handouts or suggestions for family activities to follow up on the meeting topic.

- Use language familiar to the audience and avoid jargon.

Encourage Active Participation

- Small-group discussions are the ideal. Groups of three to five people usually work best.

- After introducing a topic for discussion, it's a good idea to have each group appoint a reporter who will take notes to share later with the larger group.

- Avoid lectures lasting more than ten minutes or so. Present information when appropriate, but don't monopolize discussions. Involve the participants in discussions by stressing they have valuable experiences and ideas to share.

- Use "wait time." Ask a question, then wait. Slowly count to seven and then rephrase the question, if necessary. If you rush to answer the question yourself or call on the same outgoing person every time, the others will be less likely to participate. Try to get several different answers to each question.

- Don't ask parents to speak, read, or write unless they volunteer. Respect the right to pass. Respect their privacy.

- Recognize that for some people listening to the discussion is a form of participation.

- Nevertheless, try to draw out quiet parents. If you accept all contributions attentively and politely, the quieter parents will realize their opinions count, too.

Handle Problems Tactfully

It's important to clarify from the beginning what the parent meetings are not. They're not designed to be gripe sessions or therapy sessions. In fact, it would be highly inappropriate for parents to discuss their home lives in public.

Make this clear at the beginning of the meetings. Try to keep discussions general, rather than talking about problems specific families are experiencing with their children. Emphasize that in describing situations the participants should avoid referring to anyone by name; instead, they can say "Someone I know . . ." or "I know of a situation where. . . ."

Be prepared for other possible problems. For example, if one or two people dominate the meeting, be sure to direct

The Skills for Growing *program encourages the entire family to get involved, and I think that is the reason it's successful.*

—Uttra Bhargava, parent, Riverview Public School, Cumberland, Ontario

The involvement of parents who had been part of the Skills for Growing *training was the key to the success of the meeting. Afterward one parent said, "This is the first meeting I've attended that gave specific ideas about how to listen to children and communicate with them at home."*

—David King, principal, Brush College Elementary School, Salem, Oregon

your questions to the group. Use eye contact or gestures to encourage specific individuals other than those who are most outspoken. If someone still monopolizes the discussion, gently but firmly interrupt, saying, "While we're on the subject, what do some of the rest of you think about that?" Or if a parent keeps interrupting, make it possible for others to speak—e.g., "Excuse me, but Mrs. Thomas didn't get to finish. Let's hear what she has to say."

It's also best if you sense a potential argument to head it off at the pass. A parent might disagree with something you or someone else suggested, for example, and present reasons why the suggestion won't work. Agree with the parent that all approaches can't apply in all cases. If appropriate, ask others if they have experienced a similar problem and found a way to handle it. If a parent suggests solving conflicts by physical force, encourage discussion of alternatives. Never imply that the approach you're suggesting is the only right one, however. Encourage parents to describe other ways they show effective listening behavior, solve problems, or handle a particular situation.

If the discussion becomes emotional or highly charged, try to express understanding and acknowledge speakers' points of view. You could say, for example, "It sounds like you're concerned about . . . ," or you could ask if others have found ways to handle similar situations.

Evaluate the Meetings
An evaluation form for both the leader and the parents has been provided for each meeting. Feedback from these forms can be helpful in planning future meetings.

Celebrating Cultural Diversity

Depending on your community, participants at parent meetings may represent a wide range of cultures and ethnic groups, each with its own traditions and communication style. Because encouraging and strengthening communication between parent and child is an important goal of the Lions-Quest *Skills for Growing* program, leaders must respect and be sensitive to established family patterns. Often this means realizing that not all parents view education and schools in the same way. In addition, *Skills for Growing* celebrates the positive elements of the wide variety of cultures represented in our schools and communities.

Strengthening Home-School Relationships

Your team can play a leadership role in strengthening home-school relationships by encouraging all school staff to be knowledgeable about and sensitive to the various ethnic and cultural groups in the community. One way to do this would be to ask for help from local community leaders, colleges, and universities. They might provide information and training, for example, in such topics as multicultural communication skills, cultural differences in parenting, and ways to promote the involvement of parents from different cultures and groups.

Identifying community leaders who reflect the cultural diversity of the community will be a key to such efforts. They, in turn, can help to reach and involve parents from their respective ethnic groups. They can also help determine the needs and expectations of parents in the community and take them into account in planning the parent meetings.

Skills for Growing celebrates the positive elements of the wide variety of cultures represented in our schools and communities.

Many parents have special needs that will make it difficult for them to get involved.

The Special Needs of Low-income Parents

Many parents may have special needs that will make it difficult for them to get involved in a school program. Currently 9.5 million households in the United States are headed by a single female; 16 percent of these parents are under age 25, 50 percent are unemployed, and 42 percent live in central cities. Twenty-five percent of the children who entered school in 1985 live in poverty; for blacks the figure is 50 percent and for Hispanics, 40 percent (Lezotte 1985).

Parents in such situations are unlikely to attend a parent meeting or become involved in school programs if they are having trouble dealing with other needs that are more basic. In some communities helping parents become aware of appropriate services and agencies may be a higher priority at first than getting them to come to a *Skills for Growing* meeting. Being aware of these primary needs can be crucial in building trust with some parents, and it can lead to their later involvement in school-related activities.

A telephone network of bilingual volunteers can be helpful.

Taking Account of Differences in Language

In situations where parents may have problems speaking or understanding English, be certain to provide information in a variety of ways: pictures and graphics, repetition of ideas using different words, and translations, when appropriate. A telephone network of bilingual volunteers can be helpful in inviting parents and getting comments from those who may not speak out at meetings.

When planning a parent meeting, consider the need for the following approaches:

- Conducting the meeting in one language only
- Presenting the meeting in two languages by having a bilingual leader or leaders who can speak and interpret both languages

- Having translators available for each language group expected at the meeting

If you use interpreters, their skill and familiarity with the *Skills for Growing* program will be a factor in the success of the meeting. We recommend that interpreters complete the *Skills for Growing* training or at least observe several parent meetings beforehand.

Make sure to emphasize in your telephone calls, fliers to community organizations, posters, and invitations that one of these approaches will be used.

The Importance of Appreciating Differing Cultural Values

While leading the parent meetings and interacting with parents from different cultures, keep in mind the following areas of cultural difference.

- Time concepts. Differences here can lead to misunderstandings about punctuality and "taking turns."
- Eye contact. In some cultures avoiding direct eye contact with a person in a position of authority is a sign of respect.
- Gestures. The meaning of a certain gesture may vary from one culture to another. For example, some cultures consider touching the top of a child's head insulting; in others crossing one's legs is offensive.
- Personal space. Some cultures encourage people to stand or sit close to each other. Others discourage closeness, especially between the sexes.
- School and teachers. Many cultures hold teachers in high esteem and assume they know best. In others, formal education may not be considered as important as other values.
- Individual vs. group effort. Some cultures value individual work and achievement, while others feel one's efforts should benefit the larger group.
- Sense of control. In some cultures children are taught that they are responsible for what happens in their lives. In others they learn their future is determined or

We're seeing a ripple effect that is carrying over beyond the Skills for Growing *groups in class. They are finding solutions by working together. They might watch 16,000 hours of TV during their lives, and often what they see is a violent, unkind response. But we have groups of children learning to talk. That carries over to families and neighborhoods after school.*

—Mary Johnson, principal, St. Ann School, Lansing, Illinois

strongly influenced by one or more external factors over which they have little or no control.

- Male and female roles. This can affect the interaction between the meeting facilitator and a parent of the opposite sex.
- Holidays. The dates for parent meetings should be selected carefully to avoid conflict with traditional family holidays.

To work effectively with people from diverse cultures, you'll need to have a basic understanding of differing customs and traditions. If you're in doubt about the culture and traditions of your school's community, this information may be available from community leaders who represent various population groups.

At times, in both *Skills for Growing* classes and your parent meetings, there may be differences between skills the program teaches and the culture of specific groups or participating parents. You need to be sensitive to this possibility and take it into account. For example, you may want to say at appropriate points, "In some cultures there may be other ways of doing this. We're trying to teach our students to respect and understand many different cultures. We recognize that children may do some of these things in different ways at home, and we respect that."

Including the Community

Most communities have a variety of resources that can be tapped for the benefit of children, families, and schools. Lions Clubs, the PTA, civic and fraternal groups, health- and youth-oriented agencies, clergy, business people, and many others can become valuable allies to help with the parent meetings and support the Lions-Quest *Skills for Growing* program generally.

Community involvement in *Skills for Growing* creates reciprocal relationships. The community can help support and strengthen the program. In turn, the program can make positive contributions to the community as it encourages children to seek productive roles through service learning projects and as it creates a climate for open communication and cooperation among families, the school, and the community.

In addition, families, schools, and communities working together transmit a message of unity that gives children and youth a clear understanding of adult expectations.

"The reason no one listens to us is because we don't pay taxes."

Involving Lions Clubs and the PTA

Repeatedly in this guide we refer to ways you can involve your local Lions Club and PTA. Keep in mind that these two leading national organizations are major co-sponsors of *Skills for Growing*. Their national leadership has spread the word about *Skills for Growing* and regularly encourages members to become involved. You can help stimulate this involvement by reaching out to Lions Clubs and the PTA when it's appropriate to do so.

Lions Clubs and the National PTA are major co-sponsors of *Skills for Growing*.

Choosing a Community Liaison

The teams trained to implement the *Skills for Growing* program often include parents, Lions Club members, and

Lions helped bring everything together for us.

—Sandy Pineda, principal, Maryland Avenue Demonstration School, La Mesa, California

We have a large PTA board, and they do most of the volunteering.

—Rex Cole, principal, Dan D. Rogers Elementary School, Dallas, Texas

other community representatives, in addition to administrators and teachers. A parent, a Lion, or a community member of a team is a logical person to serve as community liaison.

The community liaison can help with the parent meetings and the program by providing leadership at schoolwide events connected to the program, informing the community about the program, encouraging people to get involved, and helping to plan and lead or co-lead the parent meetings.

If your Implementation Team does not include a community representative, one of the members should be asked to act as the community liaison. As the program gets established at your school, your team will be in a better position to recruit a community person for this role.

Outreach for Community Support

As soon as possible, the community liaison and other members of the Implementation Team should begin to build a network of colleagues and volunteers who understand the program, want to help support it, have good contacts in the community, and will take the lead in reaching out to community resources. In addition to the team members, others who could help are teachers, PTA members, Lions, and parents whose older children are now or were students in the Lions-Quest *Skills for Adolescence* or *Skills for Living* programs.

Provide the networking group with copies of the overview handout on page 61. Ask them to contact, in person or by telephone, the leaders they know in local agencies and organizations likely to support the concepts of *Skills for Growing.*

The public library may have a directory of local organizations with names and telephone numbers of their officers or staff. The community calendar printed in daily or weekly papers is another good source of leads.

Roles for Community Representatives

Community representatives are more likely to become involved if they clearly understand what roles are available. Let them know their involvement is valued and they and members of their organizations can help by:

- Identifying and linking community resources to meet the needs of children and families
- Helping to provide positive peer group activities for children
- Organizing parent support groups
- Becoming involved as guides and sponsors in service learning projects
- Helping to organize alcohol and other drug awareness forums
- Raising funds to sponsor a special event or purchase materials
- Underwriting the cost of training additional school staff members, parents, or community volunteers
- Participating in the parent meetings

Involving Community Representatives in the Parent Meetings

For some community representatives the parent meetings may be the point of first involvement in *Skills for Growing*. If they've had children in elementary school, they can share their experiences during discussions. Those who work in fields related to education and child development may also be able to provide information. Some may be good organizers who can help establish parent support groups. Some may be able to encourage parents to come who would otherwise be reluctant.

Personal invitations to community members, followed by letters and phone calls, are an important beginning. Children in action—at the meeting or on videotape—can also be a key to getting people to attend.

I talked with our parent group, because they'd been involved in very successful fund-raising activities. I told them if they'd approve funding of the program, I would immediately approach the local Lions Club for reimbursement. We were fortunate that the husband of one of our teachers is a long-term Lions Club member. . . . He presented my letter at one of the meetings.

—Margaret-Ann Young, principal, Aldergrove Elementary School, Edmonton, Alberta

Community involvement completes the network of support for children by linking the home, the school, and the community.

Strengthening Your Partnerships

Whatever role community representatives play in the *Skills for Growing* program, maintaining their goodwill is important.

Here are some ways to strengthen your partnerships:

- Invite community members to observe *Skills for Growing* classes.
- Send them letters from students telling about progress on joint projects or thanking them for their help.
- Ask if you and possibly a group of students can make a presentation about the program at one of their meetings.
- Encourage the media to report efforts and contributions to the program from individuals and organizations in the community.
- Present them with certificates of appreciation—for example, at the completion of a project, after the last parent meeting, or at the end of the school year.
- Form an advisory committee composed of Lions, PTA members, educators, and parents who can respond to special needs that may arise. This committee can serve to keep all parties well-informed and involved.

Community involvement in the parent meetings and in every other aspect of the program completes the network of support for children by linking the family, the school, and the community. It will be worth the extra effort and time it requires.

Forming Family Support Groups

O nce you've held your first series of Lions-Quest *Skills for Growing* parent meetings, you may discover that some participants feel a need to continue meeting and sharing information. A family support group can serve this purpose.

Many family support groups simply provide friendship among people who share similar situations. Others are organized around a specific concern or issue.

A family support group offers parents the comfort of learning they aren't alone. Through a support group, parents can gain information about common problems, a sense of hope that these problems can be dealt with, knowledge of available referral sources, and help in developing skills to cope more effectively.

Finding Effective Support Group Leaders

The parent meeting leader or other members of the *Skills for Growing* team may be asked to help establish a parent support group. Unless you have the time and willingness to take on this responsibility, one response would be to offer to serve as a resource to get the group started. The team could also survey community representatives to locate an appropriate leader. An alternative would be to set up a system of shared or rotating leadership. People who have a high level of energy and commitment often move into leadership roles.

"Mrs. Horton, could you stop by school today?"

A successful group meets a need. Begin by asking what is already available for parents.

Questions to Ask Before Starting a Support Group

A successful family support group meets a need. The following questions can be helpful in considering setting up a support group:

- What is already available in the community for parents? What gap in existing services would be filled by a new support group?

- What function would the group have? Peer support? Social? Growth/self-improvement? Education? Community action?

- Would the group focus on a specific topic, such as alcohol and other drugs, single parenting, or raising a handicapped child? Or would the group deal with a variety of issues and needs?

- Would the group move toward independence from both the *Skills for Growing* program and the school? If so, who would lead the group?

- What relationship would the *Skills for Growing* team have to the group?

Establishing a Family Support Group

The following steps can be helpful in establishing family support groups:

Step 1: Identify a core group

This group would accept the main responsibility for organizing the support group and make a commitment to follow through. Ideally its members will already have been involved in the *Skills for Growing* parent meetings and indicated an interest in follow-up activities.

Step 2: Assess needs

This might include determining the goals of the group, finding out the expectations of the potential members, and gathering ideas about meeting times, dates, and locations.

Step 3: Develop a plan

Planning might include:

- Developing a statement of purpose, ground rules for the meetings, and perhaps a philosophy statement
- Locating a meeting place
- Selecting a regular day and time to meet

Step 4: Recruit members

The group leaders could begin by inviting all parents who have been taking part in the *Skills for Growing* parent meetings. Recruitment could also be done through a telephone network. Parents who have already indicated an interest could be encouraged to bring a friend.

Step 5: Plan the first meeting

Planning for the meeting might include deciding on a topic and inviting a guest speaker to discuss it; organizing a literature table with materials from community resources; designing a handout with information about the group and subsequent meetings; and finding translators or interpreters, if necessary.

Step 6: Conduct the meeting

Stay close to your agenda, but recognize the importance of giving the participants enough time to interact. You might want to end the meeting, like the parent meetings described in this guide, with a social time. (Note that following the descriptions of the three parent meetings we present guidelines for setting up your own parent meetings. You may find these guidelines helpful in planning and conducting meetings of various kinds of family support groups.)

Remember that family support groups may be organized for social purposes as well as to share concerns. Parents whose children are classmates or friends may want to spend time getting to know the families of those children. Support groups can serve a variety of purposes and should be allowed to evolve in a natural way in response to real needs.

Family support groups may be organized for social purposes as well as to share concerns.

Building Family Communication Skills

Overview

Goals

1. To inform parents about the Lions-Quest *Skills for Growing* program and have them experience some of the classroom activities.

2. To discuss the importance of good family communication and share ideas to enhance communication.

3. To encourage parent-to-parent interaction and support.

Time

Ninety minutes, with additional time for refreshments. If you wish to shorten the meeting to about an hour by deleting some of the activities, those items marked by an asterisk could be omitted.

The Meeting at a Glance

1. Welcome the participants. (3 minutes)

2. Review the topics, goals, and agenda. (2 minutes)

3. Complete a "Get Acquainted" activity. (15 minutes)

4. Describe the *Skills for Growing* program. (10 minutes)

5. Introduce a *Skills for Growing* listening activity. (25 minutes)

Stretch—2 minutes

Read over all the suggested activities several days before the session. The schedule is full but flexible. Omit any activity that may not be appropriate for this particular parent group. Be certain to allow time for interaction and discussion. Enabling parents to share ideas and reactions is more important than covering all the material.

"Because being a student is your societal role. That's why you have to go to school."

*6. Complete an activity to encourage good family communication. (20 minutes)

*7. Identify community resources. (5 minutes)

8. Summarize the meeting. (5 minutes)

9. Fill out evaluation forms. (5 minutes)

10. Provide refreshments and a social time.

Preparation

1. Make name tags and charts.

2. Prepare handouts, refreshments, and a comfortable seating arrangement.

3. Plan for child care.

4. Display work done by students (optional).

Materials

1. Name tags, chalkboard, chalk, chart paper, easel, tape, markers

2. Overhead projector

3. Handouts

- Lions-Quest *Skills for Growing* Overview (page 61)
- Listening Skills
- Using "Why" Messages to Improve Family Communication
- Expressing Appreciation to Family Members
- Community Resources (to be developed by leader, time permitting)
- Meeting Evaluation Form

4. Copies of *Together Times*

5. Charts (see boxes in meeting description)

- The Three Parent Meetings
- Goals of Parent Meeting One, "Building Family Communication Skills"

- Meeting One Agenda
- Let's Get Acquainted
- Listening Skills
- The Three Parts of a "Why" Message
- "Blaming" Messages vs. "Why" Messages
- Vague vs. Specific Messages of Appreciation

6. Overhead masters

- Five Program Components
- Classroom Curriculum
- Parent and Community Involvement
- *Together Times* Student-Family Activity Booklets

7. Sign-up sheets

- School Climate Committee
- Classroom Volunteer
- Networking Groups/Task Forces
- *Skills for Growing* Team Training
- Service Projects Volunteer

8. Media (optional)

- Slides or videotape about the *Skills for Growing* program available from Quest International

If you are interested in ordering the slides or video-tape, contact Quest International at:

Toll-free:	
Canada	800/265-2680
Ohio	800/233-7900
USA	800/446-2700
Outside USA (this is a toll call)	614/522-6400

Student involvement can be a powerful incentive for parents to attend.

Description of Activities

Student Involvement

Student involvement in the parent meetings can be a powerful incentive for parents to attend. For this meeting students could lead a listening activity from a *Skills for Growing* lesson, perform a skit, act as greeters, or hand out materials. The children would need their own activities, such as a video or games, for the time they are not part of the meeting.

1. Welcome the participants. (3 minutes)

Welcome everyone warmly. Introduce yourself, the principal, any other members of the *Skills for Growing* team, and special guests.

2. Review the topics, goals, and agenda. (2 minutes)

The words in italics serve as your script for the parent meeting. You may want to adapt these words for your own situation.

This is the first of three parent meetings that are a key part of the Parents as Partners component of the Lions-Quest Skills for Growing *program. The first meeting focuses on the topic "Building Family Communication Skills." The three meetings are based on the same topics children learn about in* Skills for Growing *classes.*

Show Chart 1, "The Three Parent Meetings."

Chart 1

The Three Parent Meetings

Meeting One: Building Family Communication
                 Skills

Meeting Two: Positive Prevention—Thinking
                 Ahead

Meeting Three: Celebrating the Family

This meeting will help the group review different approaches for improving communication in the family. During the meeting we'll discuss and apply communication skills that can be used at home. You'll all have opportunities to interact with each other and share your own insights and experiences.

Show Chart 2, "Goals of Parent Meeting One, 'Building Family Communication Skills,' " and read the goals to the group.

Chart 2

Goals of Parent Meeting One
"Building Family Communication Skills"

1. To inform parents about the Lions-Quest *Skills for Growing* program and have them experience some of the classroom activities.

2. To discuss the importance of good family communication and share ideas to enhance communication.

3. To encourage parent-to-parent interaction and support.

People are born with only two things. The first is potential; the second is an environment in which that potential may be developed. For most people in the family, it is the environment in which the majority of the development occurs.

—H. Stephen Glenn, *Developing Capable Young People*

Within nuclear families with two parents present, interaction has been reduced to fourteen and one-half minutes per day. Of these . . . over twelve are used in one-way, negatively toned communication—parents issuing warnings or reproving children for things done wrong.

—H. Stephen Glenn, *Developing Capable Young People*

Our parents enjoyed the interaction. They broke into small groups, each with a Skills for Growing teacher. They liked learning something they could take home. The children gave demonstrations and sang a song about respecting each other.

—Phil Donk, counselor, Ganado Elementary School, Ganado, Arizona

We had several presenters, so it wasn't too much for any one person. Two trained parents helped with the opening activities, and several staff members presented the rest.

—Betty Matwichuk, assistant principal, Aldergrove Elementary School, Edmonton, Alberta

Show Chart 3, "Meeting One Agenda."

Chart 3

Meeting One Agenda

Let's Get Acquainted: Activity

About Lions-Quest *Skills for Growing*

The Gift of Listening: Activity

Communicating with "Why" Messages

Community Resources

Summary and Evaluation

Refreshments

After getting acquainted with each other, you'll participate in some activities similar to those your children experience in the classroom. Since this meeting focuses on family communication, the major emphasis will be on effective listening and communicating with "Why" messages as a way of solving problems and conflicts. We will also explore ways to express clear and specific messages of appreciation to family members.

There will be a two-minute stretch, and everyone is welcome to stay for refreshments after the meeting.

3. Complete a "Get Acquainted" activity. (15 minutes)

If there are more than 30 people, divide the large group into smaller ones for these introductions.

The goals of the parent meetings include parent-to-parent support and linking the resources of the home, the school, and the community. To do this, it will help if we get to know each other better by introducing ourselves.

Unit One of Skills for Growing *emphasizes feeling comfortable and valued as part of the classroom and school community. Our names are important to us, and children feel more comfortable in the classroom when they're called*

by the names they like. To give everyone a chance, each introduction will be limited to 30 seconds. I'll give you a signal at the end of each 30-second introduction period.

Show Chart 4, "Let's Get Acquainted."

Chart 4

Let's Get Acquainted

The name you like to be called

Your child's name or nickname

Your child's teacher's name

A favorite family activity

During your 30 seconds you'll introduce yourself, say your child's name, give the name of your child's teacher, and mention a favorite family activity. Those of you who don't have children at the school can share a favorite family activity you remember as a child.

If children attend the meeting, have them participate in the activity, too. They'll have to introduce themselves within the 30-second time limit as part of their parent's sharing time.

Allow time for the introductions. Then bring the group together for closure.

Closure

- *Think about one thing you have in common with others at this meeting.*
- *Would anyone like to share something you just thought about?*

For any schoolwide event two invitations are sent home. One is for the family and one for neighbors who may be senior citizens or couples without children.

—Walter Krahn, principal, Langley Meadows Elementary School, Langley, British Columbia

I liked the sharing and frank discussion. It would be beneficial, I think, if parents could come together like this more often—"Skills for Parenting"!

I liked the willingness of the parents to share their ideas, feelings, and perceptions.

I hope this will continue. Let me know how I can help.

—Anonymous comments from parents on evaluation forms after a parent meeting at Madison Elementary School, Newark, Ohio

Overhead 1

Five Program Components

Classroom Curriculum

Training

Parents As Partners

Skills for Growing

Community Involvement

Positive School Climate

57

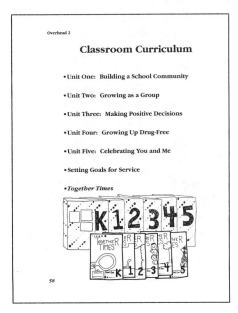

Overhead 2

Classroom Curriculum

• Unit One: Building a School Community

• Unit Two: Growing as a Group

• Unit Three: Making Positive Decisions

• Unit Four: Growing Up Drug-Free

• Unit Five: Celebrating You and Me

• Setting Goals for Service

• *Together Times*

58

4. Describe the *Skills for Growing* program. (10 minutes)

Instead of describing the program through the narration outlined here, you may want to show the slide presentation or videotape about the program available from Quest International.

Lions-Quest Skills for Growing *is a joint program of four key organizations: Lions Clubs International, the National Association of Elementary School Principals (NAESP), the National PTA, and Quest International. Major contributors to the program are the W.K. Kellogg Foundation, JCPenney and the Moore Foundation.*

Parents as Partners is one part of the larger program. This comprehensive program for grades K-5 brings together parents, educators, and members of the community to teach children important life skills within a caring and consistent environment. The program teaches skills in four main areas:

- *Self-discipline*
- *Responsibility*
- *Good judgment*
- *Getting along with others*

A basic aim of the program is to develop a support system for children that involves the home, the school, and the community working together.

Referring to Overhead 1, "Five Program Components," describe the five main parts of the program.

Classroom Curriculum. *The curriculum offers lessons for an entire year for each grade level, K-5. All the lessons use a variety of ways to teach social and academic skills. The five units of the curriculum, each with a distinct theme, are repeated at each grade level.*

Now show Overhead 2, "Classroom Curriculum," and make the following points:

The curriculum contains five units.

- *Unit One: Building a School Community*
- *Unit Two: Growing as a Group*
- *Unit Three: Making Positive Decisions*
- *Unit Four: Growing Up Drug-Free*
- *Unit Five: Celebrating You and Me*

Also included in the Curriculum Guides is a process for planning and carrying out a school or community service project. Service projects help teach children the value of serving others by learning through doing. You may have already heard about service projects in which your children were involved. They can be as simple as writing letters to pen pals and as complex as a project to beautify the school grounds.

Another important part of the curriculum is the use of the Student-Family Activity Booklets, Together Times. We'll come back to these in a moment.

Show Overhead 1 again and continue the presentation. To bring the presentation to life, include examples of actual events and activities that are part of your own *Skills for Growing* program.

Positive School Climate. *Developing and enhancing a positive school climate—making school a positive, happy experience for everyone involved—is a key goal of* Skills for Growing. *Toward this end, the program creates a School Climate Committee whose main function is to organize a series of schoolwide events throughout the year related to the program goals and curriculum themes. These events help to extend the impact of the program beyond the classroom and throughout the school. Everyone is invited to participate, and themes often include such aspects of the program as friendship, families, cooperation, and school spirit.*

Parents as Partners. *The series of three parent meetings is a key element in the parent component. Other ways you can become involved include activities in the Student-Family Activity Booklets, Together Times; participation on the School Climate Committee; and support and sponsorship for service learning projects.*

One of the most effective ways to enhance the climate of schools is to involve parents at all levels of school life. Parents . . . bring to schools valuable insights and unique perspectives, which serve to enhance home-school relationships, student behavior, and academic achievement.

—Norris M. Haynes, James P. Comer, and Muriel Hamilton-Lee, "School Climate Enhancement Through Parental Involvement," *Journal of School Psychology*, vol. 27, 1989

The program helps to create a spirit of cooperation that brings the school and community closer together.

Community Involvement. *For community members the program helps to create a spirit of cooperation that brings the school and community closer together. Community involvement builds support in the community not just for the school but for children and families in general. It can range from funding for training and materials provided by community groups to the participation of community members in a variety of program activities, such as school climate events and service projects.*

Training and Follow-up Support. *A group called the Implementation Team carries out the program at each school and begins the process by going through an indepth training workshop. The training offers an introduction to the five components of the program and experience with innovative teaching techniques and the program materials. Follow-up support is available through supplements that highlight new ideas from* Skills for Growing *classrooms. Assistance is also provided through a toll-free phone line.*

How to get involved. *The parent meetings are designed to support parents as their children's first teachers. The meetings offer an opportunity to exchange ideas with parents of your children's friends, get to know others in the school and community better, learn about the program, and discuss and practice ways to reinforce skills the program teaches within the family.*

If the members of this group would like to increase their involvement in the program beyond the parent meetings, we welcome you to become more active in several ways.

Show Overhead 3, "Parent and Community Involvement."

Briefly describe the various ways parents and community members can become involved in the program, providing examples of the types of experiences they are likely to have in the program at your school. Emphasize that sign-up sheets will be available at the end of the meeting if the participants want to become involved in the *Skills for Growing* program in any of these ways.

Now introduce *Together Times*. Display several copies or show Overhead 4, "*Together Times* Student-Family Activity Booklets," as you make the following points:

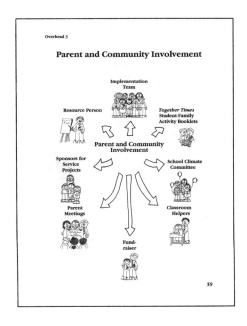

Each student receives a copy of Together Times *for each unit in the curriculum.*

- Together Times *was designed to be fun, involving, and interactive by offering students interesting activities to do. The booklets reinforce skills the students are learning in the units.*

- *In addition to helping students learn skills taught in the curriculum, each copy of* Together Times *reinforces skills in reading, writing, listening, and speaking.*

- *After the students have completed activity sheets in* Together Times *in class, they take their copies home as a gift to their families. Additional activity sheets and articles are provided for families to do and read at home.*

- Together Times *is a unique teaching tool designed to bring the school and home closer together. All parents should expect to see their children's copies of* Together Times *at the end of each unit—approximately every four to six weeks.*

- *In every issue a place is provided where parents can respond with comments, suggestions, and notes. Please be sure to let us know your reactions and thoughts by sending a message to your child's teacher in the special space designed for that purpose.*

Hand out the *Skills for Growing* Overview from page 61. Give the group a few minutes to look at it. An alternative would be to hand out copies as people enter the meeting room and ask them to glance through it while they're waiting for the meeting to begin.

Ask if anyone has questions or comments. If some questions will be answered during other parent meetings, refer the group to Chart 1 to indicate when that topic will be covered.

5. Introduce a *Skills for Growing* listening activity. (25 minutes)

Good family communication is a key to raising healthy, responsible children. Communication skills are a main focus of the first two units of Skills for Growing.

Good family communication is a key to raising healthy, responsible children.

"Your computer says! Your computer says! When I was your age, I quoted my father."

Listening skills include actions—what you do—and responses—what you say.

In Unit One children learn basic rules of consideration and respect for others—how to make the classroom an orderly place where people know and care about each other.

In Unit Two they learn and practice listening skills. They learn to show that they're listening both by their actions—what they do—and by their responses—what they say.

Show Chart 5, "Listening Skills."

Chart 5

Listening Skills

Actions (What You Do)	Responses (What You Say)
Look at the speaker	Encourage the speaker to continue
Pay attention	Ask questions
Show you're listening through facial expressions, eye contact, etc.	Rephrase or summarize
Sit forward and nod	Make comments

Actions include looking at the speaker, paying attention, and showing you're listening through facial expressions, eye contact, and so on. Responses include encouraging the speaker to continue, asking questions, rephrasing or summarizing what the speaker has said, and making appropriate comments. Children in grade five learn and practice all these skills, and children in the earlier grades learn a few of them at a time. They're skills that can be useful for adults, too.

Keep in mind that listening behaviors differ among cultures. You may have parents from cultures where avoiding direct eye contact is a sign of respect, especially with people in positions of authority—such as teachers. If this is a possibility, do not insist upon eye contact or present it as an essential listening behavior. Emphasize that in the *Skills for Growing* program students are encouraged to learn about and respect many different cultures and ways of listening and interacting.

For the following skit you'll need to choose an adult or student volunteer beforehand to play the role of the Parent. Play the part of the Neighbor yourself.

In a moment you're going to experience a listening skills activity similar to those done in the Skills for Growing classroom. But first [volunteer's name] and I are going to demonstrate the kind of communication that occurs when people do not use listening skills. As you watch the skit, think about the consequences of my behavior as I play the part of a poor listener. [Volunteer's name] is a parent who has just received some exciting news in the mail; I'm a neighbor who happens to be nearby when [he/she] opens the mail that day.

Enact the following situation.

In *Skills for Growing* students are encouraged to learn about and respect many different cultures and ways of listening and interacting.

Situation

The last time the Parent went shopping with his/her family they entered a drawing for a new bike. The Parent just received a letter in the mail announcing his/her family is the lucky winner and they can come to the store next Saturday to pick up the bike. The Parent is very pleased that his/her youngest child will now have the kind of bike she's been wanting. The Parent sees the Neighbor and goes over to share the good news.

The Neighbor is a poor listener. As the Parent goes on in an excited way, instead of using listening skills, the Neighbor looks away in a bored manner, yawns, interrupts, and so on.

Good schools attract partners. They communicate regularly with their community. They produce newsletters to parents, take surveys of needs and wants, maintain telephone contact, and sponsor workshops. Some schools arrange for weekly newspaper columns on radio and television reports about school activities. They also have learned to make use of their cable access. They consciously involve their community in solving problems and shaping curriculum needs. They look carefully at their community to see who can help.

—"A Look at America's Great Schools," *Instructor,* Special Issue, Fall 1986

After you've presented the skit, emphasize that in the classroom children practice only positive behaviors and the teacher demonstrates the inappropriate behavior if that's required.

Ask:

- *What did the Neighbor say that made you think he/she was a poor listener? What did he/she do?*
- *What effect do you think the Neighbor's behavior had on the Parent?*
- *How do you think people in general feel when they're not listened to?*

Distribute copies of the handout "Listening Skills." If children are taking part in the meeting, they can participate as partners with adults in the following activity. You may wish to have them demonstrate listening skills from a classroom lesson.

Now I'd like each of you to pair up with someone you don't know well and decide who will be numbers one and two. This time your goal will be to practice the listening skills we've already discussed. Each pair will take turns playing the role of speaker and listener. You can refer to the "Listening Skills" handout or the chart as a reminder of the kinds of skills to use. Feel free to take the handout home and display it for the whole family to see.

We'll take one minute for the first conversation, during which the "ones" will be the speakers and the "twos" the listeners. Then I'll signal that it's time to switch roles, and you'll have one minute for the second conversation. Each time the speaker will talk about what you enjoy most about your family. Listeners, remember to use listening skills as your partners talk.

Serve as the timekeeper. After one minute, signal the group and ask them to reverse roles. Allow one more minute to complete the second conversation.

Observe the pairs during the activity. Then give the group feedback about the listening skills you saw and heard.

Bring the group together for closure.

Closure

- *How did you feel telling your partner something about your family? What helped you to share this information?*
- *What specific behaviors and words indicated your partner was listening?*
- *Was it easier to do the talking or the listening? Explain.*
- *How can you apply what you've experienced here with your family?*

Stretch—2 minutes

At this point you may wish to have the children move to another room where you've provided child care, videos, cooperative games, and other activities. You may also wish to take this time for an appropriate energizer.

6. Complete an activity to encourage good family communication. (20 minutes)

Welcome back. In addition to learning how to be listeners, students in Skills for Growing classes learn to communicate effectively by using "Why" messages. Students learn about "Why" messages in Unit Two, mainly in kindergarten and grades three and four.

"Why" messages help to communicate clearly and directly. They're a helpful way of dealing with problems and conflicts. In Skills for Growing, children discover there are several ways of handling a conflict:

- *One is just to let it pass, which may be a good thing to do when the conflict isn't very important or serious.*
- *Another is to try to hurt the other person through blaming, teasing, or some other inappropriate means—children often handle conflicts this way.*
- *The third is to try to solve the problem constructively, and one way to do this is with a "Why" message.*

"Why" messages allow us to tell others in a positive and helpful way how their behavior affects us and why the behavior is a problem. They help suggest another behavior that will improve the situation. They help to avoid "Blaming" messages, which often make the situation worse. "Why" messages help us to express ourselves while opening channels of communication with others.

The main way for young people to develop interpersonal skills is to be in relationships in which those skills are used and demonstrated. Such a relationship is characterized by sharing feelings. As a person develops the ability to identify personal feelings and cope with them productively, he or she begins to recognize that others share these same feelings, frustrations, and challenges. On this building block the skills for communication, cooperation, negotiation, sharing, and intimacy are built.

—H. Stephen Glenn, *Developing Capable Young People*

The statements on this and the following page were written by students at Aboite Elementary School, in Fort Wayne, Indiana, when they were asked to say what they were learning in their *Skills for Growing* classes.

My brother and I got in a fight, and I used my "Why" messages and told him, "I don't like it when you hog the Nintendo!" He responded, "Do you want to play two players?" I said, "Yes."

In Skills for Growing we learn a lot of things we will need when we grow up. I really think we will keep this for a long time, like math and reading, because when I grow up and have kids I hope they will have this advantage of life.

I liked it when we learned how to talk to a person without getting mad. A person in my math class always gets mad when I was nice to her. Now we are OK friends.

I feel the Skills for Growing program helped me learn how to be a better listener and how not to play the blame game.

A "Why" message, as it's taught to students in Skills for Growing classes, has three parts.

Show Chart 6, "The Three Parts of a 'Why' Message."

Chart 6

The Three Parts of a "Why" Message

Name the behavior that's bothering you.

Say why the behavior is bothering you.

Say what you'd like to happen instead.

One part is to name the behavior that's bothering you. Another is to say why the behavior is bothering you. And a third is to say what you'd like the person to do instead. You can say them in any order—it's not a precise formula or series of steps to follow.

Here's an example of a "Why" message for a negative situation that's probably familiar to many of us: "When you leave your toys in the hall, people step or fall on them, so please put them in your room after you've finished playing."

Here's another: "When you don't come home right away after school, I worry that something may have happened to you. Come home right away or call me and let me know what you're doing."

In family situations "Why" messages can be a good alternative to "Blaming" messages, which tend to begin with "You . . ." and often lead to "blocked" communication, with both parties ending up hurt, angry, or resentful. "Why" messages can help to avoid blaming, and they can be a positive, constructive tool for solving conflicts.

Let's take a moment to compare "Why" messages with "Blaming" messages and discuss the effects each one might have on the attitudes and behaviors of others.

Show Chart 7, " 'Blaming' Messages vs. 'Why' Messages."

Chart 7

"Blaming" Messages vs. "Why" Messages

"Blaming" Messages	"Why" Messages
You always procrastinate! You didn't clean up your room when I told you to. Go do it.	I asked you to clean up your room and you haven't done it yet. It's important to me to have a clean house when we're having company. I need to know when you plan to do it, since it has to get done before company arrives.
You're always forgetting things! You should have called to say you'd be late. How would you like it if someone did that to you?	I'm really upset that you didn't call to tell me you'd be late. Please let me know next time so I can make plans.

What do the "Blaming" messages communicate? How would most people react?

Threats and put-downs generally make people feel defensive and angry. They act as blocks to communication. In encouraging more effective and open communication in families, one goal is to make it clear that we disapprove of a person's behavior, not the person.

Post a sheet of chart paper. Ask for volunteers to give examples of typical situations that might occur at home for which a "Why" message might be appropriate. Give some examples yourself if people seem reluctant to volunteer suggestions.

I learned how to give compliments to people. When I was at home I was just about to hit my brother when I used a "Why" message.

After Skills for Growing I feel more confident of myself! My brother and I used to get in a lot of fights. But now they are narrowed down to about 1 fight every 3 weeks. My family and I get along now that Skills for Growing is in my family.

I like Skills for Growing because I think people can learn to be nice to others and respect others.

This program has really helped me have a better relationship with my family.

I like Skills for Growing because it helps me be a better friend. It also helps me have more friends. Now I have lots more friends than I used to have.

I think our class has been a better class because of this program. It makes me want to come to school when I'm sick.

Encourage the group to try using "Why" messages with their children.

Now model the use of "Why" messages by giving examples of the three parts for one of the situations listed on the chart paper.

Ask everyone to choose a partner. Allow four minutes for them to practice using "Why" messages. They can use the examples on the chart paper or make up their own. Be sure to let the group know when two minutes is up so both partners have an opportunity to share.

Bring the group together for closure.

Closure

- *Think of one way "Why" messages could help things go better at home.*
- *Raise your hand if you would like to share what you're thinking.*
- *Think about something that might make it hard for you to use "Why" messages at home.*
- *Would anyone like to share some potentially difficult situations?*

Distribute copies of the handout "Using 'Why' Messages to Improve Family Communication." Encourage the group to save the handout, post it at home, and try using "Why" messages with their children.

In Unit Two of Skills for Growing *children also learn and practice ways to express appreciation to others—friends, family, school staff, and so on. This helps to build the climate of cooperation and positive communication that's one of the main objectives of the first two units. A key communication concept taught in Unit Two that can be useful at home is the idea of vague versus specific messages when expressing appreciation.*

Show Chart 8, "Vague vs. Specific Messages of Appreciation."

Chart 8

Vague vs. Specific Messages of Appreciation

Vague	Specific
You're great.	You're always thoughtful about other people—that's great!
Super job.	Thanks for cleaning up afterward.
You look good.	Those colors look terrific on you.

As parents it's helpful to say what we appreciate about our children rather than making unclear statements. When we give vague messages we sometimes encourage kids just to please us without having a clear idea what they've done that they should be proud of. Specific messages of appreciation help to define behavior that's acceptable; they give more guidance than vague messages.

Distribute copies of the handout "Expressing Appreciation to Family Members."

You may find this handout helpful at home. It describes some of the same ways to express appreciation children learn in Skills for Growing classes. Also, it will help to serve as a reminder of the important difference between vague and specific messages of appreciation.

Note that you can express appreciation for a variety of things. These include appearance, effort, skills, and specific behavior.

Appreciation can be expressed for a variety of things—appearance, effort, skills, and specific behavior.

We have a group of ten parents who went through the training, and they've been a key to parent involvement. They're called the Parents as Partners Committee. We decided to do that as soon as we knew we were going to adopt the program. . . . One of the main benefits is these parents have been going through the same kinds of experiences with their children as the other parents we want to involve. They're well-prepared, and the other parents see them as credible. It builds a real sense of positive support for the program. . . . Now we have parents saying, "These teachers really know what they're talking about," and teachers are saying, "It's really great that parents are taking the time for this."

—David King, principal, Brush College Elementary School, Salem, Oregon

Closure

- *Think of an example of a clear and specific message of appreciation for a family member, based on something you observed in your family recently. Think of how to express this as a specific message instead of a vague one.*
- *Who would like to share with the group the message you were thinking of?*
- *What makes the message clear and specific?*

7. Identify community resources (5 minutes)

Refer the group to resources in the community either by providing a handout or, if time is limited, asking group members to suggest five or six organizations or agencies of special value to families.

If time allows, hand out your list of names, addresses, and phone numbers of local organizations that offer information and services for children and families. If possible, have pamphlets or fliers from these organizations on display. Make sure the agencies reflect the ethnic and cultural makeup of the community.

To get started, you might call a local Lions Club, the PTA, the Chamber of Commerce, Boys and Girls Clubs, the YM/YWCA, 4-H Clubs, and Scouts. Check the library for a list of local organizations, or look in the yellow pages under "family," "health," and "recreation."

You might invite representatives from one or more of these local organizations to attend the meeting or come for refreshments and an opportunity to talk with the group afterward.

Ask the participants to think about other organizations to suggest at the next meeting.

8. Summarize the meeting. (5 minutes)

Now, thinking back on the meeting, turn to someone nearby and share two thoughts or two new pieces of information you'll take home as a result of this meeting. You'll have two minutes for this exchange.

Bring the group together and ask:

- *What have you enjoyed most about this meeting?*
- *What is one thing you might do differently as a result of this meeting?*
- *Think about something you learned at this meeting that's different from how your family does things. Similar to how your family does things.*
- *Would anyone like to share what differences or similarities you learned about?*

Remind the group of the date and time of the next meeting.

Beware of "Fall-Off"! Encourage Continuing Participation

In order to encourage parents to attend the next meeting and remain involved, make sure to highlight some kind of special event or activity as part of the next meeting. This might range from bringing their child's favorite snack to planning a potluck. You may also wish to organize a special presentation by students.

Announce the event or activity at the end of this meeting. Encourage the participants to spread the word and bring others, and follow up with posters, announcements, and publicity.

9. Fill out evaluation forms. (5 minutes)

Ask the group to complete the meeting evaluation form. You and others on the organizing team may wish to complete the form for meeting leaders so you can compare your reactions and plan for future meetings.

"My parents aren't perfect, but I have quite an emotional investment in them."

10. Provide refreshments and a social time.

Invite the group to stay for refreshments and a social time. Be sure to encourage the participants to sign up for the different roles they can take in the program. Post the sign-up sheets where they will be easy to see.

Five Program Components

Classroom Curriculum

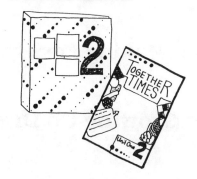

Training

Parents As Partners

Skills for Growing

Community Involvement

Positive School Climate

Classroom Curriculum

- **Unit One: Building a School Community**

- **Unit Two: Growing as a Group**

- **Unit Three: Making Positive Decisions**

- **Unit Four: Growing Up Drug-Free**

- **Unit Five: Celebrating You and Me**

- **Setting Goals for Service**

- ***Together Times***

Parent and Community Involvement

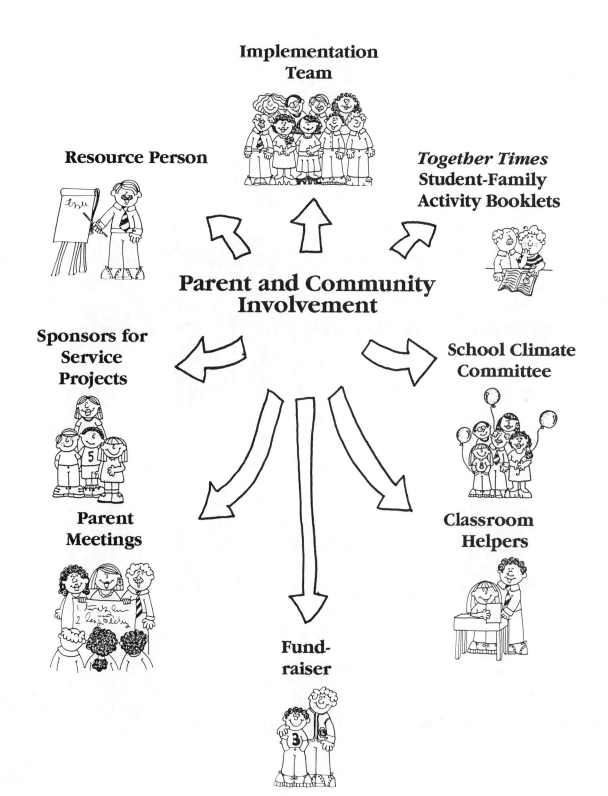

Implementation
Team

Resource Person

Together Times
Student-Family
Activity Booklets

**Parent and Community
Involvement**

Sponsors for
Service
Projects

School Climate
Committee

Parent
Meetings

Classroom
Helpers

Fund-
raiser

Together Times
Student-Family Activity Booklets

One per student per unit

Fun, interactive

Reinforce skills taught in the units

Reinforce skills in reading, writing, speaking, and listening

Activity sheets to be completed at school

Presented as a gift to families at the end of the unit

Lions-Quest *Skills for Growing*

Overview

Lions-Quest *Skills for Growing* has been made possible by the support of four key organizations: Lions Clubs International, the National Association of Elementary School Principals (NAESP), the National PTA, and Quest International. Major donors to the program are the W.K. Kellogg Foundation and JCPenney.

Skills for Growing is a comprehensive program for grades K-5 that brings together parents, educators, and members of the community to teach children important life skills within a caring and consistent environment. The program teaches skills in four main areas:

- Self-discipline
- Responsibility
- Good judgment
- Getting along with others

A basic aim of the program is to develop a support system for children that involves the home, the school, and the community working together.

The program has five main parts:

Classroom Curriculum. Children may participate in *Skills for Growing* lessons for an entire year at each grade level, K-5. All the lessons offer a variety of ways to teach social and academic skills. The curriculum contains five units that are repeated at each grade level, each with a distinct theme. The units and their main themes are:

- Unit One: Building a School Community
- Unit Two: Growing as a Group
- Unit Three: Making Positive Decisions
- Unit Four: Growing Up Drug-Free
- Unit Five: Celebrating You and Me

Also included in the Curriculum Guides is a process for planning and carrying out a school or community service project. Service projects help teach children the value of serving others by learning through doing.

Important to each unit are the activities in the *Together Times* Student-Family Activity Booklets. These booklets reinforce what children learn in *Skills for Growing* classes. The booklets also contain activities and information for families to enjoy together at home. At the end of each unit the children take their booklets home as a gift to their families.

Positive School Climate. Developing and enhancing a positive school climate—making school a positive, happy experience for everyone involved—is a key goal of *Skills for Growing*. Toward this end, the program creates a School Climate Committee whose main function is to organize a series of schoolwide events throughout the year related to the program goals and curriculum themes. These events help to extend the impact of the program beyond the classroom and throughout the school. Everyone is invited to participate, and themes often include such aspects of the program as friendship, families, cooperation, and school spirit.

Parents as Partners. The series of three parent meetings is a key element in the parent component. Other ways of involving parents include activities in the Student-Family Activity Booklets, *Together Times*; parent participation on the School Climate Committee; and parent support and sponsorship for service learning projects.

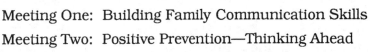

The three parent meetings are designed to support parents as their children's first teachers. The meetings offer an opportunity for parents to exchange ideas with parents of their children's friends, get to know people in the school and community better, learn about local resources, and discuss and practice how to increase communication within the family. The topics of the parent meetings are:

Meeting One: Building Family Communication Skills

Meeting Two: Positive Prevention—Thinking Ahead

Meeting Three: Celebrating the Family

Community Involvement. For community members the program helps to create a spirit of cooperation that brings the school and community closer together. Community involvement builds support in the community not just for the school but for children and families in general. It can range from funding for training and materials provided by community groups to the participation of community members in a variety of program activities, such as school climate events and service projects.

Training and Follow-up Support. A group called the Implementation Team carries out the program at each school and begins the process by going through an in-depth training workshop. The training offers an introduction to the program and experience with innovative teaching techniques and materials. Follow-up support is available through supplements that highlight new ideas from *Skills for Growing* classrooms. Assistance is also provided through a toll-free phone line.

Listening Skills

One of the keys to good family communication is the ability to listen well. The *Skills for Growing* program focuses on two major listening skills: actions and responses.

Actions include what you do, such as looking at the speaker, paying attention, and showing you're listening through facial expressions, eye contact, and so on.

Responses include the things we say, such as encouraging the speaker to continue, asking questions, and rephrasing or summarizing what the speaker has said.

About Actions

Pay attention without fidgeting, looking at your watch, or looking away.

Use appropriate body posture to show your interest in what is being said. Sitting forward, nodding, and making appropriate facial expressions can all communicate interest.

About Responses

Ask open-ended questions. Asking questions also allows you and the speaker to clarify points. Open-ended questions might include:

- Can you tell me more about that?
- How did you feel about that?
- What do you think would happen if you did that?
- What help do you need?
- What do you like about that?
- How would you improve or change things?

Rephrase or summarize what the speaker has said. By rephrasing or summarizing, you indicate the message was heard and understood. The speaker also has the opportunity to clarify points if you don't rephrase them accurately.

Examples of rephrasing or summarizing statements:

- It sounds as if you felt frustrated because no one would listen to your side of the story.
- It seems as if you wanted to share your ideas, and other people were interrupting you.
- I can understand how thrilled you were to be chosen for that part in the play.

Make comments that reflect your concern or interest in a topic.

- I'd like to know more about that.
- How exciting!
- I wish I'd tried that.

Using "Why" Messages to Improve Family Communication

One way of communicating clearly and directly is to use "Why" messages. This form of communication allows us to tell others in a positive and helpful way how their behavior affects us and suggest another behavior that will improve the situation.

A "Why" message, as it's taught to students in *Skills for Growing* classes, has three parts:

· Name the behavior that's bothering you.

· Say why the behavior is bothering you.

· Say what you'd like to happen instead.

Examples:

· I asked you to tell me where you were going, and you left without letting me know. I need to know where you are. Please make sure you leave me a note before going out.

· I had no idea you were in trouble. It concerns me when you don't tell me what's happening with you. Please let me know these things, and I'll always do what I can to help you.

· You didn't write down the phone message, and that call was very important to me. If I'm not home, please write down a message for every call you answer.

Expressing Appreciation to Family Members

Vague vs. Specific Messages of Appreciation

A vague message is unclear; it doesn't say specifically what you appreciate. Try whenever possible to use specific messages, naming a particular behavior or quality.

Vague	Specific
You're nice.	I like your sense of humor.
Good job.	Thanks for being so careful.
You're helpful.	The kitchen looks great! Thanks.

Remember to Express Appreciation for . . .

We can express appreciation for many different qualities in children. These include:

- Their appearance

- Specific behavior

- Special efforts they make

- New skills they've learned

Think of examples and give your child a clear message of appreciation as often as you can.

Sample Letter to Parents Whose Children Are Enrolled in the *Skills for Growing* Program

It may be appropriate to translate this letter into languages other than English. Also, you may wish to mention in the letter that other languages will be spoken or interpreters will be present, if appropriate.

Dear Parent(s):

I'd like to invite you to three special parent meetings here at _____(school)_____. The meetings are part of the Lions-Quest *Skills for Growing* program that your child attends.

Skills for Growing is designed to help students become more self-confident, communicate better with their families, make decisions based on facts rather than pressure from their friends, and say "No" to drugs and alcohol.

The parent meetings will explain some of the important skills your child is learning through this program. They'll also give you the opportunity to discuss how to strengthen family communication. You'll have a chance to talk with other parents and share the joys and concerns of raising elementary-age children.

The meeting topics are:

Meeting 1: Building Family Communication Skills _____(date)_____

This meeting will offer ideas for improving family communication and give you a chance to practice using new skills.

Meeting 2: Positive Prevention—Thinking Ahead _____(date)_____

The focus of this meeting will be on how to prepare your child for the challenge of alcohol, other drugs, and negative peer pressure. No, it's not too early to start! Many children feel some pressure to try alcohol and other drugs by grade four.

Meeting 3: Celebrating the Family _____(date)_____

Today's parents lead busy lives. This meeting will offer some positive and interesting ways to make the most of the precious time you have with your children.

We hope you'll be able to attend all three meetings. We'll meet at _____ from ____ to ____. We've planned child care during the meetings and refreshments afterward, so please plan to stay. There is no charge.

Please fill out the following form and return it to me by _____(date)_____. If you need transportation, please call _____(phone number)_____. I look forward to sharing an exciting evening with you!

Sincerely,

Parent Meeting Response Form

I (we) will (will not) be able to attend these parent meetings:

Will be
able to
attend

Will not
be able to
attend

_____   _____   **Meeting 1: Building Family Communication Skills**

_____   _____   **Meeting 2: Positive Prevention—Thinking Ahead**

_____   _____   **Meeting 3: Celebrating the Family**

_____
(Parent's name)

_____
(Child's name)

_____
(Address)

_____
(Phone)

I (we) will need child care for _____ children, ages _____

Please check if you will need transportation: _____

Please return this form to _____ by _____

Sample Letter to Parents Whose Children Are Not Enrolled in the *Skills for Growing* Program

It may be appropriate to translate this letter into languages other than English. Also, you may wish to mention in the letter that other languages will be spoken or interpreters will be present, if appropriate.

Dear Parent(s):

I'd like to invite you to three special parent meetings here at _____(school)_____.
The meeting topics are:

Meeting 1: Building Family Communication Skills _____(date)_____

This meeting will offer ideas for improving family communication and give you a chance to practice using new skills.

Meeting 2: Positive Prevention—Thinking Ahead _____(date)_____

The focus of this meeting will be on how to prepare your child to handle the challenge of alcohol, other drugs, and negative peer pressure. No, it's not too early to start! Many children feel some pressure to try alcohol and other drugs by grade four.

Meeting 3: Celebrating the Family _____(date)_____

Today's parents lead busy lives. This meeting will offer some positive and interesting ways to make the most of the precious time you have with your children.

The meetings will provide information and guidance to help families raise children who are healthy, self-confident, and able to resist negative influences, including pressures to use alcohol and other drugs.

Attending the meetings will also give you an opportunity to meet with other parents and share the joys and concerns of raising elementary-age children.

I hope you'll be able to come to all three meetings. The meetings will be held at _____ from _____ to _____. We'll have child care during the meetings and refreshments afterward, so please plan to stay. There is no charge.

Please fill out the following form and return it to me by _____date_____. If you need transportation, please call _____(phone number)_____. I look forward to sharing an exciting evening with you!

Sincerely,

Parent Meeting Response Form

I (we) will (will not) be able to attend these parent meetings:

Will be
able to
attend

Will not
be able to
attend

_____   _____   **Meeting 1: Building Family Communication Skills**

_____   _____   **Meeting 2: Positive Prevention—Thinking Ahead**

_____   _____   **Meeting 3: Celebrating the Family**

_____
(Parent's name)

_____
(Child's name)

_____
(Address)

_____
(Phone)

I (we) will need child care for _____ children, ages _____

Please check if you will need transportation: _____

Please return this form to _____ by _____

Meeting Evaluation Form for Leaders

Meeting One: Building Family Communication Skills

1. How would you rate the success of this meeting?

1	2	3	4	5
Unsuccessful				Very successful

2. What parts of the meeting were most successful?

_____

_____

3. What parts of the meeting were least successful?

_____

_____

4. What changes would you suggest in the content of the meeting?

_____

_____

5. What changes would you suggest for the meeting guide, charts, overheads, or hand-outs?

_____

_____

6. Other comments:

_____

_____

Meeting Evaluation Form for Parents

Meeting One: Building Family Communication Skills

We want to know what you liked and did not like about this meeting. Please let us know by filling out this page.

1. I thought the meeting was (please circle one number):

1	2	3	4	5
Not Helpful				Very Helpful

2. The thing I liked best about the meeting was:

_____

_____

3. I liked the way the leader:

_____

_____

4. I wish the leader had:

_____

_____

5. The next time you have this meeting, make this change:

_____

_____

6. I would also like to learn more about:

_____

_____

Positive Prevention—
Thinking Ahead

Overview

Goals

1. To inform parents about the Lions-Quest *Skills for Growing* program and have them experience some of the classroom activities.

2. To discuss how students in *Skills for Growing* classes are learning to make positive decisions and resist pressures to engage in negative behavior.

3. To provide accurate information about drug use and ways to help children stay drug-free.

4. To establish guidelines for talking with the family about drugs.

Time

Ninety minutes, with additional time for refreshments. If you wish to shorten the meeting to about an hour by deleting some of the activities, the items marked by an asterisk could be omitted and the others shortened somewhat.

The Meeting at a Glance

1. Welcome the participants. (3 minutes)

2. Review the topics, goals, and agenda. (2 minutes)

* 3. Complete a "Get Acquainted" activity. (10 minutes)

4. Briefly describe the *Skills for Growing* program and the previous meeting. (5 minutes)

5. Define the program's approach to the prevention of alcohol and other drug use. (15 minutes)

Read over all the suggested activities several days before the session. The schedule is full but flexible. Omit any activity that may not be appropriate for this particular parent group. Be certain to allow time for interaction and discussion. Enabling parents to share ideas and reactions is more important than covering all the material.

"The cow jumped over the moon? Steroids, right?"

*6. Introduce skills, concepts, and information taught in Units Three and Four. (10 minutes)

Stretch—2 Minutes

7. Introduce facts about alcohol and other drugs and discuss how families can teach children to say "No" to drugs. (30 minutes)

*8. Summarize the meeting by discussing guidelines for talking with the family about drugs. (10 minutes)

9. Fill out evaluation forms. (5 minutes)

10. Provide refreshments and a social time.

Preparation

1. Make name tags and charts.

2. Prepare handouts, refreshments, and a comfortable seating arrangement.

3. Plan for child care.

4. Display work done by students (optional).

Materials

1. Name tags, chalkboard, chalk, chart paper, easel, tape, markers, pencils

2. Overhead projector

3. Handouts

- Lions-Quest *Skills for Growing* Overview

- Information Packet that includes the following handouts:

  — Alcohol, Other Drugs, and Youth: Understanding the Problem

  — How Can I Talk with My Family About Drugs?

  — Drug Facts

  — Teaching Your Child to Say "No" to Drugs

- Meeting Evaluation Form

4. Charts (see boxes in meeting description)

- Goals of Parent Meeting Two, "Positive Prevention—Thinking Ahead"
- Meeting Two Agenda
- Let's Get Acquainted
- Guidelines for Talking with the Family About Drugs

5. Overhead masters

- Lions-Quest *Skills for Growing* at a Glance
- *Together Times* Student-Family Activity Booklets
- The Extent of the Problem: Part I
- The Extent of the Problem: Part II
- Unit Three: Making Positive Decisions
- Unit Four: Growing Up Drug-Free

6. Sign-up sheets

- School Climate Committee
- Classroom Volunteer
- Networking Groups/Task Forces
- *Skills for Growing* Team Training
- Service Projects Volunteer

"Just say 'No' to drugs but not to spinach."

Description of Activities

Student Involvement

Student involvement in the parent meetings can be a powerful incentive for parents to attend. For this meeting students could lead an activity from a *Skills for Growing* lesson from Unit Three or Four, perform a skit, act as greeters, or hand out materials. The children would need their own activities, such as a video or games, for the time they are not part of the meeting.

. Welcome the participants. (3 minutes)

Welcome everyone warmly. Introduce yourself, the principal, any other members of the Lions-Quest *Skills for Growing* team, and special guests.

2. Review the topics, goals, and agenda. (2 minutes)

The words in italics serve as your script for the parent meeting. You may want to adapt these words for your own situation.

This is the second of three parent meetings that are a key part of the Parents as Partners component of the Lions-Quest Skills for Growing *program. This meeting focuses on information about positive prevention—how families can help children resist negative peer pressure and other influences that might hurt their health and well-being, especially influences to use alcohol and other drugs. We call this "positive prevention" because just teaching students to say "No" isn't enough. They need to be motivated to resist negative pressures and to grow up healthy and drug-free.*

Show Chart 1, "Goals of Parent Meeting Two."

Chart 1

Goals of Parent Meeting Two
"Positive Prevention—Thinking Ahead"

1. To inform parents about the Lions-Quest *Skills for Growing* program and have them experience some of the classroom activities.

2. To discuss how students in *Skills for Growing* classes are learning to make positive decisions and resist pressures to engage in negative behavior.

3. To provide accurate information about drug use and ways to help children stay drug-free.

4. To establish guidelines for talking with the family about drugs.

Show Chart 2, "Meeting Two Agenda."

Chart 2

Meeting Two Agenda

Let's Get Acquainted: Activity

About Lions-Quest *Skills for Growing*

The Need for Drug Abuse Prevention in the Elementary Grades

What Students Are Learning About Making Decisions and Saying "No"

Knowing the Facts About Drugs: Activity

Guidelines for Talking with the Family About Drugs: Activity

Summary and Evaluation

Refreshments

The program backs what we're trying to teach. My son is learning to say "No" to peer pressure and do what he feels he should do in a given situation. He doesn't necessarily go along with the crowd.

—Jennie Schlenker, parent, Meeteetse Consolidated Schools, Meeteetse, Wyoming

The meeting focuses on information about alcohol and other drugs and ways families can teach children to resist negative influences.

After getting better acquainted with each other, you'll participate in some activities similar to those your children experience in the classroom. We'll discuss information about alcohol and other drugs, and then, since children are exposed frequently to influences that pressure them to make unhealthy choices, we'll examine ways families can teach their children how to resist negative or unhealthy influences. Then we'll list guidelines for talking to children about drugs.

There will be a two-minute stretch, and everyone is welcome to stay for refreshments after the meeting.

3. Complete a "Get Acquainted" activity. (10 minutes)

If there are more than 30 people, divide the large group into smaller ones for these introductions.

The goals of the parent meetings include parent-to-parent support and linking the resources of the home, the school, and the community. To do this, it will help if we get to know each other better.

Show Chart 3, "Let's Get Acquainted."

Chart 3

Let's Get Acquainted

Your name

Your child's name

Your child's teacher's name

A free or inexpensive activity for children available in the community

---

For our activity you'll spend the next five minutes moving around the room introducing yourselves to as many people as possible and telling each one about a free or inexpen-

sive activity you recommend for children of elementary school age. An important part of teaching children to say "No" to drugs is for parents and members of the community to work together in giving them a firm, consistent "no use" message. At the same time, families and communities need to offer children positive alternatives to drug use—something to say "Yes" to.

Before we begin, take a moment to think about healthy activities for children that are available in the community.

During your introduction say your name, the name of your child and his or her teacher, and one free or inexpensive activity you recommend. You'll each have 30 seconds to introduce yourselves, and I'll give you a signal at the end of each 30-second introduction period.

If children attend the meeting, have them participate in the activity, too. They'll have to introduce themselves within the 30-second time limit as part of their parent's sharing time.

Allow time for the introductions. Then bring the group together for closure.

Closure

- *Did anyone meet a parent of a friend of your child for the first time?*
- *What were some of the most interesting activities you heard about from other parents?*
- *Were any community resources—organizations, agencies, or clubs, for example—mentioned in your conversations? If so, what were they? If not, can we name two or three that sponsor positive activities for children?*

Parents and members of the community need to work together in giving a firm, consistent "no use" message.

4. Briefly describe the *Skills for Growing* program and the previous meeting. (5 minutes)

Be prepared to make this presentation if it's appropriate. However, if the group is essentially the same as it was for the first parent meeting, you may wish to shorten the presentation or skip it altogether. For participants who were not involved in the previous meeting, you could make available copies of the program overview on page 61.

Lions-Quest Skills for Growing *is a joint program of four key organizations: Lions Clubs International, the National Association of Elementary School Principals (NAESP), the National PTA, and Quest International. Major contributors to the program are the W.K. Kellogg Foundation, JCPenney and the Moore Foundation.*

Parents as Partners is one part of the larger program. This comprehensive program for grades K-5 brings together parents, educators, and members of the community to teach children important life skills within a caring and consistent environment. The program teaches skills in four main areas:

- *Self-discipline*
- *Responsibility*
- *Good judgment*
- *Getting along with others*

Show Overhead 1, "Lions-Quest *Skills for Growing* at a Glance."

To bring the presentation to life, include examples of actual events and activities that are part of your own *Skills for Growing* program.

Classroom Curriculum. *The curriculum offers lessons for an entire year for each grade level, K-5. All the lessons use a variety of ways to teach social and academic skills. The five units of the curriculum, each with a distinct theme, are repeated at each grade level.*

Also included in the Curriculum Guides is a process for planning and carrying out a school or community service project. Service projects help teach children the value of serving others by learning through doing. A service project can be as simple as writing letters to pen pals and as complex as a project to beautify the school grounds.

Another important part of the curriculum is the use of the Student-Family Activity Booklets, Together Times. We'll come back to these in a moment.

Positive School Climate. *Developing and enhancing a positive school climate—making school a positive, happy experience for everyone involved—is a major goal of Skills for Growing. Toward this end, the program creates a School Climate Committee whose main function is to organize a series of schoolwide events throughout the year related to the program goals and curriculum themes. These events help to extend the impact of the program beyond the classroom and throughout the school. Everyone is invited to participate, and themes often include such aspects of the program as friendship, families, cooperation, and school spirit.*

Parents as Partners. *The parent meetings are a key element in the parent component. Other ways of involving parents include activities in the Student-Family Activity Booklets, Together Times; parent participation on the School Climate Committee; and parent support and sponsorship for service learning projects.*

Community Involvement. *For community members the program helps to create a spirit of cooperation that brings the school and community closer together. Community involvement builds support in the community not just for the school but for children and families in general. It can range from funding for training and materials provided by community groups to the participation of community members in a variety of program activities, such as school climate events and service projects.*

Training and Follow-up Support. *A group called the Implementation Team carries out the program at each school and begins the process by going through an in-depth training workshop. The training offers an introduction to the five components of the program and experience with innovative teaching techniques and the program materials. Follow-up support is available through supplements that*

Service projects help teach children the value of serving others.

Parents and community members can become involved in a variety of ways.

highlight *new ideas from* Skills for Growing *classrooms. Assistance is also provided through a toll-free phone line.*

If the members of this group would like to increase their involvement in the program beyond the parent meetings, there are several ways to become more active. These include attending training, serving on the program's School Climate Committee, volunteering in the classroom, sponsoring service projects, participating in networking groups, and sharing the Together Times *Student-Family Activity Booklets with family members at home. Sign-up sheets will be available at the end of the meeting if you wish to become involved in related program activities.*

Display several copies of *Together Times* and show Overhead 2, "*Together Times* Student-Family Activity Booklets," as you make the following points:

- *Each student receives a copy of* Together Times *for each unit in the curriculum.*

- Together Times *was designed to be fun, involving, and interactive by offering students interesting activities to do. The booklets reinforce skills the students are learning in the units.*

- *In addition to helping students learn skills taught in the curriculum, each copy of* Together Times *reinforces skills in reading, writing, listening, and speaking.*

- *After the students have completed activity sheets in* Together Times *in class, they take their copies home as a gift to their families. Additional activity sheets and articles are provided for families to do and read at home.*

- Together Times *is a unique teaching tool designed to bring the school and home closer together. All parents should expect to see their children's copies of* Together Times *at the end of each unit—approximately every four to six weeks.*

- *Every issue provides a place where parents can respond with comments, suggestions, and notes. Please be sure to let us know your reactions and thoughts by sending a message to your child's teacher in the special space designed for that purpose.*

This is the second in the program's series of parent meetings. During the first meeting we introduced communication skills families can use at home that are similar to the

Overhead 2

Together Times
Student-Family Activity Booklets

One per student per unit

Fun, interactive

Reinforce skills taught in the units

Reinforce skills in reading, writing, speaking, and listening

Activity sheets to be completed at school

Presented as a gift to families at the end of the unit

94

***Together Times* is a unique teaching tool.**

skills students learn in Skills for Growing *classes. Specifically, we focused on listening skills, communicating clearly and directly with "Why" messages as a way of solving problems and conflicts, and how to express appreciation for family members.*

Ask if anyone has questions or comments.

5. Define the program's approach to the prevention of alcohol and other drug use. (15 minutes)

This section includes a good deal of information in presentation form. You may wish to introduce the information yourself or involve the group members more actively by having them read the appropriate handouts in the Information Packet aloud or share the information with a partner. If you decide to conduct the presentation as written in this guide, be sure to stop frequently and ask the group if they have any questions or comments in order to keep them actively involved.

As you present this information, be sure to ask if the participants have questions or comments—keep them actively involved.

Distribute the Information Packets.

The main focus of this meeting is on helping children avoid the temptation to use alcohol and other drugs. But before we talk about how Skills for Growing *helps prevent alcohol and other drug use among children, we need to define some terms and be clear about the nature of drug use today. One of the most important things to be aware of is the extent of the problem and how serious a threat it is even to children in elementary school. You might think drugs are only a problem at the secondary level, but that isn't so.*

Show Overhead 3, "The Extent of the Problem: Part I."

Now I'd like to provide you with some information that will help you better understand the nature of the drug problem—and think more clearly about ways to initiate positive prevention with your children at home. All of the information I am about to present is summarized in the

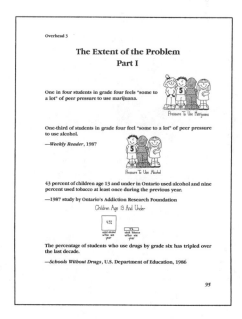

The greater the variety, frequency, and seriousness of childhood antisocial behavior before age 10, the greater the risk of persistent and frequent delinquency continuing into adulthood.

—J. David Hawkins and associates, in *Youth at High Risk for Substance Abuse*, National Institute on Drug Abuse, 1987

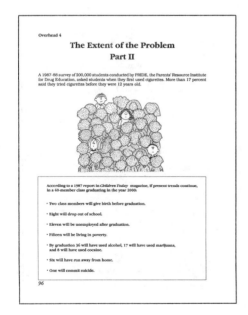

first part of Handout 1 in your Information Packet titled "The Extent of the Problem." Please keep this to refer to as you think over what you learn at this meeting.

To begin the presentation, I would like you to consider the following facts:

A 1987 Weekly Reader *poll found that one in four students in grade four feels "some to a lot" of peer pressure to use marijuana and one-third feel "some to a lot" of peer pressure to use alcohol. The pressure to use alcohol remained nearly the same in grades 4-6 and showed a steady increase through the grades, going from 36 percent in grade four to 76 percent in grades 7-12.*

A 1987 survey conducted by Ontario's Addiction Research Foundation found that 43 percent of Ontario children age 13 and under used alcohol and nine percent used tobacco at least once during the previous year.

According to a 1986 publication of the U.S. Department of Education, the percentage of students who use drugs by grade six has tripled over the last decade. In the early 1960s marijuana use was virtually nonexistent among 13-year-olds, but now about one in six 13-year-olds has used marijuana.

Show Overhead 4, "The Extent of the Problem: Part II."

A 1987-88 survey of 200,000 students conducted by PRIDE, the Parents' Resource Institute for Drug Education, asked students when they first used cigarettes. More than 17 percent said they tried cigarettes before they were 12 years old.

Experts agree that effective drug abuse prevention programs must begin no later than the elementary grades. By middle and junior high school many young people have already begun to experiment with alcohol and other drugs, and it's too late for prevention—the problems have already begun.

Research shows that if initial experimentation can be prevented up to and during the vulnerable teen years, young people are far more likely not to have problems with drugs later in life.

Finally, according to a 1987 report in Children Today magazine, if present trends continue, in a 40-member class graduating in the year 2000:

- Two class members will give birth before graduation.
- Eight will drop out of school.
- Eleven will be unemployed after graduation.
- Fifteen will be living in poverty.
- By graduation 36 will have used alcohol, 17 will have used marijuana, and 8 will have used cocaine.
- Six will have run away from home.
- One will commit suicide.

These facts are significant for all of us who are involved in the lives of children in elementary school. They clearly indicate that now is the time to start with positive prevention.

Ask if anyone has questions or comments. If any of these will be dealt with in the following presentation or activities, mention this and move on.

A key issue in preventing drug use among youth is to define what we mean by the word "drug." This word can mean different things to different people. How would you define the word "drug"?

Take a minute or so to ask volunteers to say how they would define the word "drug."

We may all have many different ideas about the meaning of "drug." These ideas will influence how we view the drug problem.

In the Skills for Growing program when we talk about drugs we're referring to many different kinds of drugs. You'll find these listed in the second section of Handout 1, "How 'Drugs' Are Presented in Skills for Growing."

One kind are medicines. Children are taught that medicines are legal and should be used only under the supervision of a trusted adult. They learn that medicines can be harmful if we use them improperly, such as using someone else's prescription drug without a doctor's advice or

Although there is no evidence to suggest that young people abuse alcohol or other drugs to a greater extent than do other age groups, the need to prevent the abuse of these substances before it begins calls for a particular focus on youth . . . and their parents.

—Government of Canada, *Action on Drug Abuse*, 1988

In addition to the physical effects . . . , a very real danger in marijuana use is its possible interference with growing up. As research shows, the effects of marijuana can interfere with learning by impairing thinking, reading comprehension, and verbal and arithmetic skills. Scientists also believe that the drug may interfere with the development of adequate social skills and may encourage a kind of psychological escapism. Young people need to learn how to make decisions, to handle success, to cope with failure, and to form their own beliefs and values. By providing an escape from "growing pains," drugs can prevent young people from learning to become mature, independent, and responsible.

—National Institute on Drug Abuse, *For Parents Only: What You Need to Know About Marijuana*, 1984

using the wrong dosage of the kind of medicine you can buy without a prescription. Students in the primary grades learn about the proper and improper use of medicines in Unit Four of the Skills for Growing curriculum.

The curriculum also teaches about other drugs that are legal for adults. Tobacco and alcohol are the two most important. Yet they are two of the most dangerous drugs available today. Together alcohol and tobacco are the cause of more accidents, deaths, and other harm to people than all the other categories of drugs combined.

Then come the drugs that are illegal for everyone— marijuana, cocaine and crack, narcotics, LSD, and so on. Students learn about all of these different kinds of drugs in Unit Four, and for all of them they learn one main idea: all drugs are potentially harmful and all but medicines are illegal for minors to use.

It's also important to know which children are at risk for problems with drugs. Research has found certain factors can cause some children to be at higher risk than children who don't experience these risk factors.

Ask the group to look at the third section of Handout 1, "Risk Factors for Alcohol and Other Drug Use." You may wish to present this information yourself, ask volunteers to read the information aloud to the group, or ask everyone to turn to a partner and share the information in pairs. The important thing is to read the needs of the group and decide if they would feel more comfortable with you presenting the material or whether they need to be more actively involved at this point.

Our society has been struggling with the drug problem for a long time. Experts believe that a key to helping children avoid drugs is to prepare them to become healthy, capable adults. That's why we've called this meeting "Positive Prevention." The fourth section of Handout 1, "Becoming the Best You Can Be," offers some suggestions for how to make this happen. All of these are emphasized in the Skills for Growing program.

Ask the group to look at the fourth section of the handout, "Becoming the Best You Can Be." Again, decide how best to engage them with the new information: presentation, reading aloud, or sharing in pairs.

Bring the group together for closure.

Closure

- *Think about something you've learned that made you realize it's important to begin positive prevention programs in the elementary grades.*

- *Who would like to share a reason why prevention programs are important in the elementary grades?*

- *What are some ways you can use this information in your own families?*

- *What concerns do you have about alcohol and other drug use among youth in the community?*

6. Introduce skills, concepts, and information taught in Units Three and Four. (10 minutes)

Keep in mind that the presence of *Skills for Growing* students, at least during the first half of the meeting, can be a critical factor in motivating parents to attend. A student demonstration of decision-making skills or skills for saying "No" would be a logical presentation to organize during this review of Units Three and Four. Make sure the students are well-prepared.

Unit Three, "Making Positive Decisions," and Unit Four, "Growing Up Drug-Free," build on skills students learn in the preceding two units. We discussed some of these skills at the previous parent meeting. Important among them are communication and listening.

Show Overhead 5, "Making Positive Decisions."

Unit Three, "Making Positive Decisions," explains the steps of decision making for different age groups. As children grow older, they add steps to the process.

You might want to have some students demonstrate decision-making skills at this point. You will also need to adapt this activity to the steps children are learning at the grade level covered in your meeting. If you've or-

> **Consider a student demonstration of decision-making skills or skills for saying "No."**

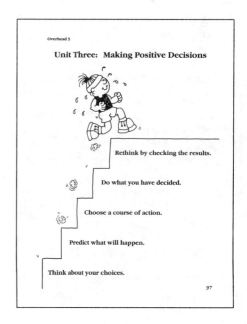

Overhead 5

Unit Three: Making Positive Decisions

Rethink by checking the results.

Do what you have decided.

Choose a course of action.

Predict what will happen.

Think about your choices.

97

ganized an all-school meeting, make it clear which steps children are learning at which grade levels.

It's important to be aware that in Unit Three students are learning how to make positive decisions about a variety of issues that affect their health and well-being—but not drug use. Skills for Growing teaches children that, where drugs are concerned, there are no viable options; instead, the only acceptable course of action is to say "No."

The reason for teaching children a decision-making process is to help them decide between choices when there is a range of positive options of equal value. An example might be giving your child a choice of whether to spend a week with his or her grandparents or a week at summer camp. Another might be how your child might spend special money he or she has received for a birthday—whether to spend it on a video game or on rides at the state fair or put it in a bank and save it.

As adults we have to guide children to know when something they're considering might be harmful or not. They're bound to encounter influences that encourage them to think some negative things are positive—advertisements for cigarettes, for instance. Children need information with which to counter these influences. They need to know that for some things the only answer is "No."

After students have discussed and practiced decision making in Unit Three, we present them with information about the harmful effects of alcohol and other drugs in Unit Four and teach them to say "No" to harmful drugs. You can reinforce this information at home—through conversations with your children about alcohol and other drugs and by using the activity pages designed for this purpose in the Together Times Student-Family Activity Booklets.

Show Overhead 6, "Growing Up Drug-Free." Explain that the lessons for all the grades convey information about the topics described in this overhead.

This would be another good place to have *Skills for Growing* students make a presentation about what they've learned in class. The presentation could include posters, artwork, writings, and other information produced by students. It could also include student demonstrations

Children need to know that for some things the only answer is "No."

Overhead 6

Unit Four: Growing Up Drug-Free

Staying healthy

Positive alternatives to harmful situations

Safety with household products and medicines

Growing Up Drug-Free

You must be 21 and show proper I.D. to purchase alcohol.

How laws protect us from harmful drugs

Saying "No" to negative influences and drug use

SURGEON GENERAL'S WARNING: Smoking By Pregnant Women May Result In Fetal Injury, Premature Birth, And Low Birth Weight.

Drugs and their effects

98

of the skill of saying "No" to negative influences. If you have students demonstrate how to say "No," make sure that they are not asked to portray the role of exerting negative pressure.

Closure

- *Think about some ways you could use the ideas presented so far to promote positive prevention at home.*
- *Who would like to share some of the ways you can do that?*
- *What do you think are some of the biggest challenges in helping children resist pressures to use alcohol and other drugs?*

Stretch—2 minutes

At this point you may wish to have the children move to another room where you've provided child care, videos, cooperative games, and other activities. You may also wish to take this time for an appropriate energizer.

"I guess I'll have to marry well."

7. **Introduce facts about alcohol and other drugs and discuss how families can help children say "No" to drugs. (30 minutes)**

Parents can play a key role in preventing the use of alcohol and other drugs by teaching their children facts about chemical substances and reinforcing the skill of saying "No" to negative influences. This part of the meeting will help you be prepared to do that at home.

Have the parents divide into small groups by calling out the letters of the word "talk." All the "T's" will be together, all the "A's" will be together, and so on.

Ask the group to find Handouts 2 and 3 in the Information Packet titled "How Can I Talk with My Family About Drugs?" and "Drug Facts."

The groups will work together to answer the questions on the "How Can I Talk with My Family About Drugs?" handout by referring to the "Drug Facts" handout. Each group should ask one or two volunteers to be the Recorder and Reporter. This is similar to how children work in groups in

Parents can play a key role in preventing the use of alcohol and other drugs by teaching their children facts about chemical substances and reinforcing the skill of saying "No" to negative influences.

The whole bunch of us parents have sat on our cans a long time. As parents, we've abdicated our responsibilities and never bothered to learn anything about drugs, so all our kids learn about them is from their peer groups. It's about time that we learn, so we can deal with and prevent the problem.

—Gerri Kalvin, Florida parent group organizer quoted in *Parents, Peers, and Pot II: Parents in Action*, National Institute on Drug Abuse, 1983

Skills for Growing *classes. After ten minutes, we'll discuss the answers together. All the information on the fact sheets is similar to what children are learning in Unit Four (grades four and five) of* Skills for Growing.

Allow time for the groups to complete the activity. Then bring the group together to discuss the answers.

Prepare for the second part of this activity by using a creative strategy of your own to form new groups of four people each.

Now we'll form new groups of four people and, for the next ten minutes, discuss how families can teach their children how to say "No" to drugs.

Turn to Handout 4 in your packet titled "Teaching Your Child to Say 'No' to Drugs." For the next ten minutes try to write down at least one item of specific additional information for at least three categories of the handout in which you're especially interested. If, when the group comes together to share ideas, no one chose one of the areas, we'll brainstorm ideas together for that area. Be sure to assign someone in your group to be the Reporter to share your group's ideas.

Indicate where in the room each group is to meet.

After ten minutes signal the groups to stop their activity and have each Reporter share the group's ideas. Take some time to discuss the categories that no group chose to examine. Brainstorm a few ideas for each category and encourage the participants to make notes on their own handouts for reference.

Bring the group together for closure.

Closure

Ask each person to find a partner and, taking turns, tell about one idea presented during the report that would be good to try at home. Give each pair three minutes to share ideas.

8. Summarize the meeting by discussing guidelines for talking with the family about drugs. (10 minutes)

Ask the group to think about items they would like to see on a list of points that are important to keep in mind when talking to the family about drugs.

Suggest that for the next two or three minutes they look at the Information Packet and the notes they made on the handouts. Tell them you'll ask for volunteers to offer points for our list.

After two or three minutes, ask for suggestions. Write the points on a sheet of chart paper titled "Guidelines for Talking with the Family About Drugs." If the following main ideas from the "Teaching Your Child to Say 'No' to Drugs" handout aren't included, suggest these points and ask if the group would include them.

The main points:

- Be informed about alcohol and other drugs.
- Uphold a "no-use" stance on illegal drug use for children.
- Establish clear family policies and model desired behaviors.
- Link up with other parents.
- Reinforce decision-making skills and the skill of saying "No."
- Practice good communication.
- Strengthen self-confidence in your child.

Closure

- *Think about two new ideas from this meeting that will make it easier for you to help your child grow up drug-free.*
- *Who would like to share one or two of the ideas you thought about?*
- *What is something you might do differently as a result of this meeting?*
- *What do you think will be the biggest challenges as your children grow older and you try to help them resist negative pressures?*

All adults, whether they be mothers, fathers, school administrators, community or business leaders, policymakers or law enforcers, have to convey in a no-nonsense manner to young people their concern and disapproval of drug abuse. All adults, whatever their role, have to take a strong anti-drug stand. It is possible to create a drug-free world for the next generation.

—PRIDE Canada, *Youth and Drugs: What Parent Groups Can Do to Create Drug Resistant Communities*, 1987

Beware of "Fall Off"!
Encourage Continuing Participation

In order to encourage parents to attend the next meeting and remain involved, make sure to highlight some kind of special event or activity as part of the next meeting. This might range from a "Family Picnic" held after school or on the weekend to a "Family Traditions" potluck dinner with favorite family dishes and presentations of family traditions and customs.

Announce the event or activity at the end of this meeting, encourage the participants to spread the word and bring others, and follow up with posters, announcements, and publicity.

9. Fill out evaluation forms. (5 minutes)

Ask the group to complete the meeting evaluation form. You and others on the organizing team may wish to complete the form for meeting leaders so you can compare your reactions and plan for future meetings.

10. Provide refreshments and a social time.

Invite the group to stay for refreshments and a social time. Be sure to encourage the participants to sign up for the different roles they can take in the program. Post the sign-up sheets where they will be easy to see.

Lions-Quest *Skills for Growing* at a Glance

Classroom Curriculum

Service Learning

Together Times
Student-Family
Activity Booklets

Positive
School Climate

Skills for Growing

Training and
Follow-up Support

Parents as
Partners

Community
Involvement

Together Times
Student-Family Activity Booklets

One per student per unit

Fun, interactive

Reinforce skills taught in the units

Reinforce skills in reading, writing, speaking, and listening

Activity sheets to be completed at school

Presented as a gift to families at the end of the unit

The Extent of the Problem
Part I

One in four students in grade four feels "some to a lot" of peer pressure to use marijuana.

One-third of students in grade four feel "some to a lot" of peer pressure to use alcohol.

—*Weekly Reader*, 1987

43 percent of children age 13 and under in Ontario used alcohol and nine percent used tobacco at least once during the previous year.

—1987 study by Ontario's Addiction Research Foundation

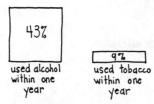

The percentage of students who use drugs by grade six has tripled over the last decade.

—*Schools Without Drugs*, U.S. Department of Education, 1986

The Extent of the Problem
Part II

A 1987-88 survey of 200,000 students conducted by PRIDE, the Parents' Resource Institute for Drug Education, asked students when they first used cigarettes. More than 17 percent said they tried cigarettes before they were 12 years old.

According to a 1987 report in *Children Today* magazine, if present trends continue, in a 40-member class graduating in the year 2000:

· Two class members will give birth before graduation.

· Eight will drop out of school.

· Eleven will be unemployed after graduation.

· Fifteen will be living in poverty.

· By graduation 36 will have used alcohol, 17 will have used marijuana, and 8 will have used cocaine.

· Six will have run away from home.

· One will commit suicide.

Unit Three: Making Positive Decisions

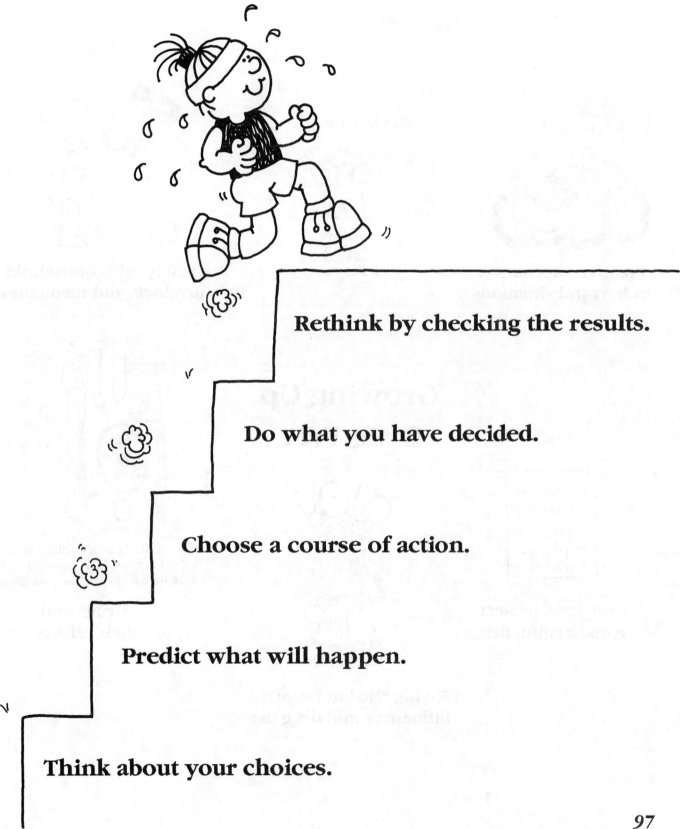

Rethink by checking the results.

Do what you have decided.

Choose a course of action.

Predict what will happen.

Think about your choices.

Unit Four: Growing Up Drug-Free

Staying healthy

**Positive alternatives
to harmful situations**

**Safety with household
products and medicines**

Growing Up
Drug-Free

You must be
21 and show
proper I.D.
to purchase
alcohol.

SURGEON GENERAL'S WARNING: Smoking
By Pregnant Women May Result in Fetal
Injury, Premature Birth, And Low Birth Weight.

**How laws protect
us from harmful drugs**

**Saying "No" to negative
influences and drug use**

**Drugs and
their effects**

Alcohol, Other Drugs, and Youth: Understanding the Problem

The Extent of the Problem

A 1987 *Weekly Reader* poll found that one in four students in grade four feels "some to a lot" of peer pressure to use marijuana and one-third feel "some to a lot" of peer pressure to use alcohol. The pressure to use alcohol remained nearly the same in grades 4-6 and showed a steady increase through the grades, going from 36 percent in grade four to 76 percent in grades 7-12.

Pressure To Use Marijuana   Pressure To Use Alcohol

A 1987 survey conducted by Ontario's Addiction Research Foundation found that 43 percent of Ontario children age 13 and under used alcohol and nine percent used tobacco at least once during the previous year.

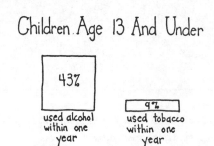

Children Age 13 And Under

43%

used alcohol within one year

9%

used tobacco within one year

According to a 1986 publication of the U.S. Department of Education, the percentage of students who use drugs by grade six has tripled over the last decade. In the early 1960s marijuana use was virtually nonexistent among 13-year-olds, but now about one in six 13-year-olds has used marijuana.

A 1987-88 survey of 200,000 students conducted by PRIDE, the Parents' Resource Institute for Drug Education, asked students when they first used cigarettes. More than 17 percent said they tried cigarettes before they were 12 years old.

Experts agree that effective drug abuse prevention programs must begin no later than the elementary grades. By middle and junior high school many young people have already begun to experiment with alcohol and other drugs, and it's too late for prevention—the problems have already begun.

Research shows that if initial experimentation can be prevented up to and during the vulnerable teen years, young people are far more likely not to have problems with drugs later in life.

According to a 1987 report in *Children Today* magazine, if present trends continue, in a 40-member class graduating in the year 2000:

- Two class members will give birth before graduation.

- Eight will drop out of school.

- Eleven will be unemployed after graduation.

- Fifteen will be living in poverty.

- By graduation 36 will have used alcohol, 17 will have used marijuana, and 8 will have used cocaine.

- Six will have run away from home.

- One will commit suicide.

How "Drugs" are Presented in *Skills for Growing*

- Medicines—drugs that can help you if they're used properly (only when supervised by a trusted adult)

- Drugs that are legal for adults but not children—alcohol and tobacco

- Drugs that are illegal for everyone—marijuana, cocaine and crack, narcotics, LSD, and so on

Risk Factors for Alcohol and Other Drug Use

- Family management problems
- Drug use by family and friends
- Failure in school
- Early antisocial behavior: stealing, fights, etc.
- Early first use
- Lack of positive ties and a sense of belonging to family, friends, school, and community
- Peers who use drugs

—Source: Professor J. David Hawkins and associates, University of Washington

Becoming the Best You Can Be

Professor J. David Hawkins, a leading authority on drug abuse prevention, has found that children need:

- Opportunities for involvement in meaningful activities

- Instruction in skills that promote involvement

- Rewards for involvement

H. Stephen Glenn, Ph.D., a key adviser to the *Skills for Growing* program, suggests children need:

· Positive self-perceptions

I am capable.

I am significant.

I can influence what happens to me.

· Skills

Self-discipline

Communicating with others

Following rules

Making good judgments

How Can I Talk
With My Family About Drugs?

Instructions: Use Handout 3, "Drug Facts," as a basis for answering the following questions.

1. A can of beer, a glass of wine, and a shot of whiskey have about the same amount of alcohol.

   True   **False**

2. Alcohol is a drug.

   True   **False**

3. Exercise and black coffee will help the effects of alcohol go away faster.

   True   **False**

4. Being in a room with a cigarette smoker can be dangerous to a nonsmoker's health.

   True   **False**

5. Smoking cigarettes can change how your body looks to other people.

   True   **False**

6. Cigarette smoking kills approximately 350,000 people a year in Canada and the U.S.

   True   **False**

7. The chemicals from marijuana can be stored in the body for as long as a month or more.

   True   **False**

8. Just one experience with cocaine or crack can lead to serious problems.

   True   **False**

9. Cocaine and crack are highly addictive. People want to use them no matter how harmful they can be.

   True   **False**

10. Sniffing inhalants can cause death.

    True   **False**

(Please cover the following when making copies.)

Answers: All are true, except number 3, which is false.

Drug Facts

This information is written so parents can discuss facts about alcohol and other drugs with children of elementary school age. The sources are listed on the last page and would be useful for families wanting more information.

Alcohol

Some Basic Facts:
- Alcohol is a drug.
- A can of beer, a glass of wine, and a shot of whiskey have about the same amount of alcohol.
- In most places it is illegal for anyone under 21 to buy or use alcohol.
- Many people do not drink alcohol at all. Others drink only a small amount at meals or special family events.

Effects on the Body:
- Alcohol is an addictive drug.
- Drinking alcohol can make a person get very sick and pass out.
- A person can die from drinking too much alcohol at one time.
- Heavy drinkers often ignore their health problems for many years.
- Alcohol can damage many parts of the body, including the brain, the stomach, and the liver.
- Alcohol drinking has a serious effect on developing children.
- The liver cleans alcohol out of the bloodstream and can be severely damaged by heavy drinking.
- When a pregnant woman drinks, some of the alcohol is passed through her blood to the baby, and this can cause serious harm to the baby.
- Exercise and black coffee can't help the body get rid of the effects of drinking. Only time will cure a hangover.

Effects on Behavior:
- Alcohol affects the brain almost immediately and can cause problems with memory, coordination, and judgment.
- Drinking doesn't make people's problems go away. It can cause new problems.
- Some people become addicted to alcohol and have serious problems with it all their lives. A person is more likely to have problems if he or she comes from a family with alcohol problems.
- Alcohol affects how people drive. Half of all car accidents are related to alcohol drinking. The leading cause of death among teenagers is car crashes in which a driver has been drinking.

Tobacco

Some Basic Facts:
- Nicotine, the main drug in tobacco, is highly addictive.
- In most places it is illegal for anyone under the age of 16 to buy cigarettes.
- Tobacco is smoked, chewed, and sniffed.

Effects on the Body:
- Smoking tobacco can cause heart disease and lung cancer.
- Tar and carbon monoxide from cigarette smoking are very damaging to the lungs and brain, causing smokers to receive less oxygen.
- Smoking deadens the taste buds on the tongue and the nerve endings in the nose that allow us to smell.
- Cigarette smoking causes stained teeth, yellow fingers, and bad breath. Other people notice these changes and find them offensive.
- Chewing tobacco can cause cancer of the mouth.
- Illness and other conditions related to cigarette smoking kill approximately 350,000 people a year in Canada and the U.S., more than for any other drug.
- Being near a smoker can make you sick. "Second-hand" smoke is dangerous to your health.
- A woman who smokes while she is pregnant risks harming her baby.

Effects on Behavior:
- Smoking tobacco can make you very nervous.
- Once a person starts smoking, it is extremely difficult to stop. This is called "addiction."
- More people today do not smoke, especially adults.
- Teenagers, especially girls, are more likely than adults to begin smoking.
- Young people who smoke usually think it won't hurt them. But they can develop all of the problems caused by smoking tobacco.
- Smoking is a major cause of fires.

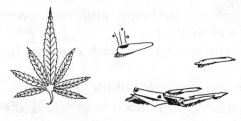

Marijuana/Cannabis

Some Basic Facts:
- It is always against the law to grow, buy, or sell marijuana, no matter how old you are.
- The marijuana leaves, and sometimes stems and seeds, are crushed and smoked or eaten.
- Marijuana contains more than 400 known chemicals. Chemicals from marijuana can be stored in the body for up to a month or more.
- The varieties of marijuana grown now are five to 20 times more powerful than those people smoked 20 years ago.

Effects on the Body:

- The effects of marijuana are subtle, long-lasting, and harmful.
- Marijuana use causes rapid heartbeat, bloodshot eyes, a dry mouth and throat, and increased appetite.
- Smoking marijuana has serious effects on the lungs.
- Using marijuana causes diseases and problems in the lungs, the brain, the heart, and the reproductive system.
- Using marijuana regularly leads to apathy and a loss of motivation.

Effects on Behavior:

- Marijuana slows down a person's reactions and makes driving dangerous.
- People who use marijuana often have a difficult time learning new information.
- Often people who use marijuana do not develop mentally as well as others who don't smoke it.
- Using marijuana can lead to serious states of depression and even psychosis.
- People who use marijuana can become lonely and unhappy. Often they become more interested in marijuana than in anything else.

Cocaine and Crack

Some Basic Facts:

- Buying, selling, and possessing cocaine is illegal.
- Cocaine and crack are highly addictive. People want to continue to use them no matter how harmful they are.
- Crack is not pure cocaine. It is mixture of cocaine and other ingredients that looks like a small, tan rock.
- Cocaine is inhaled through the nose or injected. Crack is smoked in a pipe.

Effects on the Body and Behavior:

- Cocaine is a stimulant. It makes the heart beat faster and increases the rate of breathing.
- Cocaine and crack affect the heart and brain very quickly. They cause immediate changes in the body's systems.
- Just one experience with cocaine or crack can lead to serious consequences and addiction.
- Inhaled cocaine damages the inside of the nose.
- Cocaine and crack cause sudden mood swings and affect the user's ability to think clearly.
- Cocaine and crack users lose their desire to fulfill basic needs such as eating and exercising.
- When people stop using cocaine or crack, they can become very tired and depressed.
- Use of cocaine in any form can cause death by interrupting the brain's control over the heart and lungs.

Inhalants/Sniffing

Some Basic Facts:

- Inhalants are products that can be sniffed, such as airplane glue, cooking spray, bug spray, hair spray, gasoline, nail polish remover, typing correction fluid, freon, etc.
- Chemicals including solvents and poisons are found in many common household products. They are very dangerous to breathe.
- Inhalants are inexpensive and can be bought by anyone, even children.

Effects on the Body and Behavior:

- Breathing inhalants puts harmful poisons in the lungs.
- People who sniff inhalants look as if they are drunk or having a daydream. They are likely to be dizzy and confused.
- Users often get headaches, become sick, and throw up.
- Inhalants can cause immediate and irreparable damage to the brain, the lungs, the kidneys, and the liver.
- Sniffers develop tolerance to inhalants; as time goes on, they need to use more of the chemical to get the same effect.
- Sniffing inhalants can lead to death by shutting off the sniffer's oxygen or by causing the lungs to stop working.

Sources:

National Institute on Drug Abuse. *Drug Information Pamphlet Series*. Rockville, MD: National Institute on Drug Abuse, 1986.

Addiction Research Foundation. *Facts About Drugs*. Toronto: Addiction Research Foundation, 1986.

DuPont, Robert. *Getting Tough On Gateway Drugs: A Guide for Families*. Washington, DC: American Psychiatric Press, 1984.

U.S. Department of Education. *Schools Without Drugs*. Washington, DC: U.S. Department of Education, 1987.

Ask your school or local librarian how to locate these titles.

Teaching Your Child to Say "No" to Drugs

Instructions: Here are six points families may find useful when talking to their children about drugs. With the help of the group, decide what additional information would be good to include for each point. Be as specific as possible.

1. Be informed about alcohol and other drugs and be able to discuss them knowledgeably with your child.

   a. Locate up-to-date information and share it with your family and other parents.

   b. Know the signs of alcohol or other drug use and be prepared to act if you suspect there is a problem.

   c. Know where to find help for your prevention or intervention efforts.

2. Uphold a "no-use" stance on illegal drug use for children.

   a. Set a good example by not using illegal drugs.

   b. Communicate a strong "no use" message to your children and their friends.

   c. Make it clear that illegal use of drugs will not be tolerated in your house.

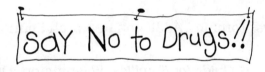

3. Set family policies and model desired behaviors.

   a. Decide on rules and logical consequences for breaking them.

   b. Demonstrate the behavior you want your children to follow.

   c. Limit the viewing of TV and movies that glamorize drug use.

4. Link up with other parents.

   a. Join a support group

   b. Know the parents of your child's friends

   c. Help establish a community drug and alcohol policy.

   d. Participate and help in community awareness programs and prevention-oriented contests, rallies, and media events.

5. Reinforce the skill of saying "No."

   a. Discuss the benefits of not using drugs and the consequences of using drugs.

   b. Discuss how it feels to say "No" to harmful situations and "Yes" to positive choices.

6. Practice good communication.

   a. Use listening skills.

   b. Find out how family members feel about a variety of issues and events in their lives.

7. Strengthen self-confidence in your child.

   a. Encourage self-discipline by setting limits and holding your child accountable for his or her behavior.

   b. Provide opportunities for your child to take responsibility in the family.

   c. Recognize and acknowledge your child's accomplishments.

   d. Let your children know you love them even when you disapprove of their behavior.

Meeting Evaluation Form for Leaders

Meeting Two: Positive Prevention—Thinking Ahead

1. How would you rate the success of this meeting?

1	2	3	4	5
Unsuccessful				Very Successful

2. What parts of the meeting were most successful?

_____

_____

3. What parts of the meeting were least successful?

_____

_____

4. What changes would you suggest in the content of the meeting?

_____

_____

5. What changes would you suggest for the meeting guide, charts, overheads, or hand-outs?

_____

_____

6. Other comments:

_____

_____

_____

Meeting Evaluation Form for Parents

Meeting Two: Positive Prevention—Thinking Ahead

We want to know what you liked and did not like about this meeting. Please let us know by filling out this page.

1. I thought the meeting was (please circle one number):

1	2	3	4	5
Not helpful				Very helpful

2. The thing I liked best about the meeting was:

_____

_____

3. I liked the way the leader:

_____

_____

4. I wish the leader had:

_____

_____

5. The next time you have this meeting, make this change:

_____

_____

6. I would also like to learn more about:

_____

_____

Celebrating the Family

Overview

Goals

1. To inform parents about the Lions-Quest *Skills for Growing* program and have them experience some of the classroom activities.

2. To explore ways to strengthen self-confidence in children.

3. To explore ways to enhance the time the family spends together.

4. To celebrate unique family activities, customs, and traditions.

Time

Ninety minutes, with additional time for refreshments. If you wish to shorten the meeting to about an hour by deleting an activity, the item marked by an asterisk could be omitted and the others shortened somewhat.

The Meeting at a Glance

1. Welcome the participants. (3 minutes)

2. Review the topics, goals, and agenda. (2 minutes)

3. Complete a "Get Acquainted" activity. (10 minutes)

4. Briefly describe the *Skills for Growing* program and the previous meetings. (5 minutes)

5. Introduce skills and concepts taught in Unit Five and lead an activity for strengthening self-confidence in children. (20 minutes)

Stretch—2 minutes

Read over all the suggested activities several days before the session. The schedule is full but flexible. Omit any activity that may not be appropriate for this particular parent group. Be certain to allow time for interaction and discussion. Enabling parents to share ideas and reactions is more important than covering all the material.

"She told me to clean out my desk, so I assumed I was fired."

*6. Discuss the importance of family time together and conduct an activity focusing on ways to make the most of the times when families are together. (20 minutes)

7. Conduct an activity about ways to celebrate family traditions. (20 minutes)

8. Summarize the meeting. (5 minutes)

9. Fill out evaluation forms. (5 minutes)

10. Provide refreshments and a social time.

Preparation

1. Make name tags and charts.

2. Prepare handouts, refreshments, and a comfortable seating arrangement.

3. Plan for child care.

4. Display work done by students (optional).

5. Arrange for special family dishes to be contributed to a "Family Traditions" potluck dinner (optional).

Materials

1. Name tags, chalkboard, chalk, chart paper, easel, tape, markers

2. Overhead projector

3. Handouts

- Treasure Hunt
- Lions-Quest *Skills for Growing* Overview
- Sources of Self-confidence
- Strengthening Self-confidence in Children
- Travel Time, Mealtime, Bedtime
- Celebrating Family Traditions
- Meeting Evaluation Form

4. Charts (see boxes in meeting description)

- Goals of Parent Meeting Three, "Celebrating the Family"
- Meeting Three Agenda
- Let's Get Acquainted

5. Overhead masters

- Lions-Quest *Skills for Growing* at a Glance
- *Together Times* Student-Family Activity Booklets

6. Sign-up sheets

- School Climate Committee
- Classroom Volunteer
- Networking Groups/Task Forces
- *Skills for Growing* Team Training
- Service Projects Volunteer

This would be an ideal time for a special "Family Traditions" potluck.

Description of Activities

Student Involvement

Student involvement in the parent meetings can be a powerful incentive for parents to attend. For this meeting students could lead an activity from a *Skills for Growing* lesson, perform a skit, act as greeters, or hand out materials. You could also display students' artwork and writings related to the themes of Unit Five.

Students could be involved in helping to prepare and carry out a "Family Traditions" potluck at the beginning or end of the meeting, and this could be especially helpful in encouraging parents to attend. The children would need their own activities, such as a video or games, for the time they are not part of the meeting.

1. Welcome the participants. (3 minutes)

Welcome everyone warmly. Introduce yourself, the principal, any other members of the Lions-Quest *Skills for Growing* team, and special guests.

2. Review the topics, goals, and agenda. (2 minutes)

The words in italics serve as your script for the parent meeting. You may want to adapt these words for your own situation.

This is the third of three parent meetings that are a key part of the Parents as Partners component of the Lions-Quest Skills for Growing *program. This meeting focuses on strengthening self-confidence in children, making the most of the time you have together as a family, and celebrating family traditions.*

Show Chart 1, "Goals of Parent Meeting Three."

Chart 1

Goals of Parent Meeting Three "Celebrating the Family"

1. To inform parents about the Lions-Quest *Skills for Growing* program and have them experience some of the classroom activities.

2. To explore ways to strengthen self-confidence in children.

3. To explore ways to enhance the time the family spends together.

4. To celebrate unique family activities, customs, and traditions.

Jerome Bruner put it simply: "We get interested in what we get good at." . . . A wise teacher starts where he or she can with each pupil. Success at something is better than no success at all.

—Theodore Sizer, *Horace's Compromise*

Show Chart 2, "Meeting Three Agenda."

Chart 2

Meeting Three Agenda

Let's Get Acquainted: Activity

About Lions-Quest *Skills for Growing*

Ways to Strengthen Self-confidence in Children

Together Times: Activity

Celebrating Family Traditions: Activity

Summary and Evaluation

Refreshments

Children are neither empty vessels to be filled with knowledge nor computers to be programmed. Rather, children actively develop their personal values and capabilities as they interact with their environment.

—Ontario Ministry of Education, *Personal and Societal Values: A Resource Guide for the Primary and Junior Divisions*

A Brown Bag Lunch for Parents

Teachers at Ridge Ranch School, in Paramus, New Jersey, prepared a brown bag lunch for parents. They took advantage of a holiday on which the schools were in session but most businesses were closed. Principal Roger Bayersdorfer commented that "The parents came and ate in the classrooms with the teachers and kids and had a wonderful time."

A Cooperative Book

As part of a service learning project at Cureton Elementary School, in San Jose, California, one class worked together to develop a cheerful storybook for a classmate hospitalized with leukemia. All the children contributed to the book, and the staff of the hospital ward shared it with their classmate.

After getting better acquainted with each other, you'll participate in some activities similar to those your children experience in the classroom. The first activity will show how we can strengthen self-confidence in children. Another will explore ways to enhance family time together. And a third will present an opportunity to share family traditions and unique characteristics.

There will be a two-minute stretch, and everyone is welcome to stay for refreshments after the meeting.

An alternative to mentioning refreshments at the end of the meeting would be to announce that the group will have an opportunity to enjoy a variety of favorite family dishes or traditions (if you've planned for this in advance).

3. Complete a "Get Acquainted" activity. (10 minutes)

The goals of the parent meetings include parent-to-parent support and linking the resources of the home, the school, and the community. To do this, it will help if we get to know each other better.

We're going to do that through a special kind of treasure hunt similar to one the students do as a get-acquainted activity in Skills for Growing. Since we're celebrating the family in this meeting, we'll all have a chance now to celebrate qualities in ourselves and at the same time get acquainted with others.

Show Chart 3, "Let's Get Acquainted," and provide everyone with a copy of Handout 1, "Treasure Hunt."

Chart 3

Let's Get Acquainted

Your name

Your child's name

Your child's teacher's name

Fill in a category

I'd like you during the next five minutes to move around the room looking for as many people as possible who have interests in the various categories listed on your "Treasure Hunt" handouts. The object is to write the name of someone else in the group in each of your squares, including a specific interest of that person, until you've filled in each category on your sheet.

For each person you find, write the person's name and his or her specific interest for that category.

Each time you meet a new person, introduce yourself, give the name of your child and your child's teacher, and then ask the person if he or she has an interest in one of the categories listed on the sheet. You may not duplicate a category until you've found at least one person for each category on the sheet. If the person doesn't have an interest in a category you need to fill in, move on to someone else and do the same thing until you've filled in your sheet completely. If there's time left, continue introducing yourself to new people and writing in a second name for the various categories.

If children attend the meeting, have them participate in the activity along with their parents as a team.

Allow five to seven minutes for the activity. Then bring the group together for closure.

Closure

- *Wave a hand if you met the parent of one of your child's friends for the first time.*

- *Think about people whose specific interests surprised or pleased you.*

- *Who would like to share something about someone else's interest that surprised or pleased you?*

Graffiti Board

At Madison Elementary School, in Newark, Ohio, students were invited to contribute to a prominently placed grafitti board on which they could write expressions of appreciation for other students and faculty members. "We change the theme from time to time," said principal Sue Smith. "It's wonderful to see the students taking this seriously and writing only positive comments."

"Cub Stubs" Celebrate Positive Behavior

At Latimer Elementary School, in San Jose, California, names of students and teachers seen doing something positive were put into classroom "pots." Once a week a drawing took place in every classroom, and the person whose name was drawn received a badge with a special design and the slogan "Show Your Pride." The school's parent organization paid for the badges.

To bring the presentation to life, include examples from your own *Skills for Growing* program.

4. Briefly describe the *Skills for Growing* program and the previous meetings. (5 minutes)

Be prepared to make this presentation if it's appropriate. However, if the group is essentially the same as it was for the first parent meeting, you may wish to shorten the presentation or skip it altogether. For participants who were not involved in the previous meeting, you could make available copies of the program overview on page 61.

Lions-Quest Skills for Growing is a joint program of four key organizations: Lions Clubs International, the National Association of Elementary School Principals (NAESP), the National PTA, and Quest International. Major contributors to the program are the W.K. Kellogg Foundation, JCPenney and the Moore Foundation.

Parents as Partners is one part of the larger program. This comprehensive program for grades K-5 brings together parents, educators, and members of the community to teach children important life skills within a caring and consistent environment. The program teaches skills in four main areas:

- *Self-discipline*
- *Responsibility*
- *Good judgment*
- *Getting along with others*

Show Overhead 1, "Lions-Quest *Skills for Growing* at a Glance."

To bring the presentation to life, include examples of actual events and activities that are part of your own *Skills for Growing* program.

Classroom Curriculum*. The curriculum offers lessons for an entire year for each grade level, K-5. All the lessons use a variety of ways to teach social and academic skills. The*

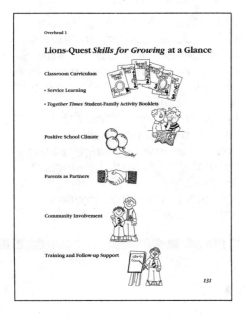

five units of the curriculum, each with a distinct theme, are repeated at each grade level.

Also included in the Curriculum Guides is a process for planning and carrying out a school or community service project. Service projects help teach children the value of serving others by learning through doing. A service project can be as simple as writing letters to pen pals and as complex as a project to beautify the school grounds.

Another important part of the curriculum is the use of the Student-Family Activity Booklets, Together Times. We'll come back to these in a moment.

Positive School Climate. *Developing and enhancing a positive school climate—making school a positive, happy experience for everyone involved—is a major goal of Skills for Growing. Toward this end, the program creates a School Climate Committee whose main function is to organize a series of schoolwide events throughout the year related to the program goals and curriculum themes. These events help to extend the impact of the program beyond the classroom and throughout the school. Everyone is invited to participate, and themes often include such aspects of the program as friendship, families, cooperation, and school spirit.*

Parents as Partners. *The parent meetings are a key element in the parent component. Other ways of involving parents include activities in the Student-Family Activity Booklets,* Together Times; *parent participation on the School Climate Committee; and parent support and sponsorship for service learning projects.*

Community Involvement. *For community members the program helps to create a spirit of cooperation that brings the school and community closer together. Community involvement builds support in the community not just for the school but for children and families in general. It can range from funding for training and materials provided by community groups to the participation of community members in a variety of program activities, such as school climate events and service projects.*

Training and Follow-up Support. *A group called the Implementation Team carries out the program at each school and begins the process by going through an in-depth training workshop. The training offers an introduction to the five*

Positive school climate activities help to extend the impact of the program beyond the classroom and throughout the school.

Together Times **was designed to be fun, involving, and interactive.**

components of the program and experience with innovative teaching techniques and the program materials. Follow-up support is available through supplements that highlight new ideas from Skills for Growing classrooms. Assistance is also provided through a toll-free phone line.

If the members of this group would like to increase their involvement in the program beyond the parent meetings, you are welcome to become more active in several ways. These include attending training, serving on the program's School Climate Committee, volunteering in the classroom, sponsoring service projects, participating in networking groups, and sharing the Together Times Student-Family Activity Booklets with family members at home. Sign-up sheets will be available at the end of the meeting if you wish to become involved in related program activities.

Display several copies of *Together Times* and show Overhead 2, "*Together Times* Student-Family Activity Booklets," as you make the following points:

- *Each student receives a copy of* Together Times *for each unit in the curriculum.*

- Together Times *was designed to be fun, involving, and interactive by offering students interesting activities to do. The booklets reinforce skills the students are learning in the units.*

- *In addition to helping students learn skills taught in the curriculum, each copy of* Together Times *reinforces skills in reading, writing, listening, and speaking.*

- *After the students have completed activity sheets in* Together Times *in class, they take their copies home as a gift to their families. Additional activity sheets and articles are provided for families to do and read at home.*

- Together Times *is a unique teaching tool designed to bring the school and home closer together. All parents should expect to see their children's copies of* Together Times *at the end of each unit—approximately every four to six weeks.*

- *The last page of each issue provides a place where parents can respond with comments, suggestions, and notes. Please be sure to let us know your reactions and thoughts by sending a message to your child's teacher in the special space designed for that purpose.*

This is the third in the program's series of parent meetings. During the first meeting we introduced communication skills families can use at home that are similar to the skills students learn in Skills for Growing classes. Specifically, we focused on listening skills, communicating clearly and directly with "Why" messages as a way of solving problems and conflicts, and how to express appreciation for family members. In the second meeting we discussed the issue of positive ways to prevent drug use. A key point was the need to begin with prevention in the elementary grades; also stressed were ways parents can teach their children to say "No" to drugs.

Ask if anyone has questions or comments.

5. Introduce skills and concepts taught in Unit Five and lead an activity for strengthening self-confidence in children. (25 minutes)

Unit Five, "Celebrating You and Me," is about appreciating the special qualities in ourselves, our families, and others. Self-confidence plays an important part in this. How would you define self-confidence? Take a moment to think about it.

After some wait time, ask for volunteers to suggest their definitions of self-confidence. Record their responses on chart paper. You might sum up by using a suggestion from the group or a definition like "belief in your own worth."

People who are self-confident experience more success in life than those who aren't. It's natural that parents want to do as much as they can to help strengthen self-confidence in their children.

Think back for a moment on your own childhood and the things that gave you a feeling of confidence in yourself. What were they? Was it a skill you learned, something you did particularly well? A person you knew who made you feel proud and special? Having an important responsibility at home or at school? Most of us can probably think back on someone or some experience that helped us feel more self-confident.

The parent meetings help with good ideas on how to communicate with your children. Today we all go in so many different directions that it's important to set up time to stay close as a family. Parents need to find out what has happened in their children's lives and share their own experiences and views.

—Sharon Bush, parent, Epperly Heights Elementary School, Del City, Oklahoma

"Teacher said we had to make 'em."

Children begin to develop a sense of themselves based on their own feelings of competence and the recognition of this competence by peers, parents, and teachers.

In the elementary school years children begin to develop a sense of themselves based on their own feelings of competence and the recognition of this competence by others—peers, parents, and teachers. Children who see themselves as capable and who feel valued develop a sense of self-respect, confidence, identity, and purpose.

Provide copies of Handout 2, "Sources of Self-confidence."

Educator Robert Reasoner has described a process for developing self-confidence in children based on many years of research involving students, teachers, and parents. This research is summarized in the handout titled "Sources of Self-confidence." Let's take a minute to review the various sources of self-confidence.

Ask for a volunteer to read the handout aloud or read it aloud yourself. Review the different sources of self-confidence and the ways adults can reinforce each one.

You can be a key factor in strengthening self-confidence in your child. Children are self-confident when they:

- *Feel capable of doing a variety of things well*
- *Feel worthwhile and important—valued, cared for, and loved by others*
- *Have some responsibility and control over the things they do and the choices they make*

Children feel self-confident when they feel capable, worthwhile, and important—also when they have some responsibility and control over the things they do and the choices they make.

Let's take the example of children's involvement in household chores. Giving your child a role in the selection of the chore will encourage a sense of responsibility and control. You can help your child feel capable by assigning chores that require some skill—and then helping your child learn the skill and master it, even if it's something like making a bed correctly or doing the laundry. When your child learns the skill and does the chore correctly, you can enhance his or her self-confidence by making specific comments about the child's accomplishment. This helps to increase your child's feeling of being worthwhile and important.

You might meet together as a family and decide who will do which chores, beginning with a discussion about what chores need to be done around the house. Other areas where children can develop a sense of competence, responsibility, and control are the preparation of meals, selection of the clothes they buy or wear, and how homework is handled. All are areas in which your child can shine. Throughout, the approach you use and the process for strengthening self-confidence are crucial.

Now we're going to break into small groups and give you a chance to talk about some of the ways you already do these things and might do more of them.

Divide the large group into small groups by using a creative strategy from the curriculum or another way to form small groups.

Give everyone a copy of Handout 3, "Strengthening Self-confidence in Children."

First take a couple of minutes to look over the "Strengthening Self-confidence in Children" handout by yourselves and think about responses for each of the three categories. Think about things you're already doing or things you might want to try. Write these down if you like. Then each group will have five minutes to brainstorm and talk about ways of strengthening self-confidence in children in each of the three categories. Each group should decide who will be the Reporter, just as students do when they work in groups in Skills for Growing classes. In about five minutes we'll come back together and the Reporters will share their groups' ideas.

Allow time for the groups to complete the activity. Then bring everyone together to share their responses to the handout.

Closure

- *Think about something you could do to strengthen self-confidence in your child that you haven't tried before.*
- *Who would like to share one of these ways to strengthen self-confidence?*
- *What new ways to strengthen self-confidence did you learn about through this activity?*

Stretch—2 minutes

Parents can help their children take responsibility for such things as the preparation of meals, the selection of their clothes, and how homework is handled.

At Aboite Elementary School, in Fort Wayne, Indiana, fourth-grade teacher Carol Nine asked the parents of her students to comment on changes they had seen as a result of their children's participation in *Skills for Growing*. On these two pages are some of their comments.

Helping others makes the kids feel needed and important. Matt's self-esteem has grown.

Brian has used compliments more with all of his family members. A lot of the skills have been practiced at home, but the reinforcement at school is a positive step for us. Through the interaction of classmates using the skills, it carries over into his relationship with the rest of us.

I like how the Skills for Growing *program has helped Rachel to be a good listener.*

At this point you may wish to have the children move to another room where you've provided child care, videos, cooperative games, and other activities. You may also wish to take this time for an appropriate Energizer.

6. **Discuss the importance of family time together and conduct an activity focusing on ways to make the most of the times when families are together. (20 minutes)**

The time we spend with our children is precious, and often we don't have enough of it. Researchers have found that in most families the parents spend only a few minutes every day interacting with their children.

Some families take time for family meetings—either in a structured way or informally at the breakfast or dinner table. This can be an excellent way to enhance family communication and appreciate each other as a family. You can have family meetings focusing on specific themes or just take time out once or twice a week to see how everyone is doing. A good idea for making family meetings work is to schedule them so they happen at the same time every week; that way, all the family members can make a commitment to be at the meeting.

In addition to family meetings or fun times that are scheduled in advance, we all have informal opportunities to strengthen family bonds. These happen most frequently during travel time, at mealtimes, and at bedtime. Suggestions for these special times can be found in the Skills for Growing *Student-Family Activity Booklets,* Together Times.

Display copies of the booklets and ask:

- *Have you tried any of these activities?*
- *What were the results?*

Allow time for the participants to share responses. You may also wish to encourage use of *Together Times* by giving some examples of these activities.

Our hectic lives today often mean parents must take advantage of time on the way to school or the babysitter, during meals, and at bedtime to talk and have fun with their children. Let's take a few moments to share with the group any of these kinds of activities you typically enjoy with your children.

Write the following headings on large pieces of chart paper or separate sections of the chalkboard:

Travel time

Mealtime

Bedtime

Ask for suggestions for each category and record them on the appropriate charts. Emphasize things to do that help to build positive social skills.

For this activity, we'll use our collective brain power to develop new ways to make the most of travel time, mealtime, and bedtime. Again, we'll divide into small groups, and each group will choose a Reporter, as in the last activity, and a Recorder, whose job is to write down people's ideas on chart paper. Both these group roles are typical of groupwork in Skills for Growing *classes.*

To divide the large group into groups of four or five, use one of the procedures that have worked for you or *Skills for Growing* teachers when dividing the students into groups in class.

Provide each group with copies of Handout 4, "Travel Time, Mealtime, Bedtime," a sheet of chart paper, some masking tape, and a felt-tip marker.

Each group's task is to brainstorm ideas for each of the three categories. In brainstorming, the main purpose is to list as many ideas as possible without discussion or judgment. After the brainstorm session we'll come back together as a large group to share your ideas. During the brainstorming each group's Recorder will write down the ideas on chart paper. Then, when we come back together to share ideas, the Reporter will tell the large group about them. You might want to use your handouts to make notes of ideas you'd like to try at home.

The Skills for Growing *program has given Pamela insight into how to treat others and deal with problems in a more relaxed and thoughtful way. The exposure children have in properly dealing with each other can only have a positive outcome.*

I like how they show self-respect and are more careful about what they say to others. Also, Angie has more self-confidence.

There is a big improvement in Scott's ability to cope with competition, friendly teasing, and sharing. He thinks more of how other people feel. It has made him more aware of problem solving and compromising.

Allow two to three minutes for the groups to brainstorm items for each category. After the brainstorm, bring everyone together to share their brainstormed lists.

Closure

- *What new ideas for family activities do you think you might try at home?*
- *What makes it hard to find quality time for your children?*
- *Think about something you've learned that might make it easier to find time together with your children.*
- *Who would like to share something you were thinking of?*

7. Conduct an activity about ways to celebrate family traditions. (20 minutes)

For our final activity we're going to celebrate some of the things that are keys to our sense of what a family is—the traditions, customs, stories, and other things that make our families unique and special to us. Every family has its own stories, games, songs, and special times that may have been passed from one generation to the next. How many of you remember family games; favorite activities; stories about aunts, uncles, cousins, or grandparents you may never have even known; or special times from childhood? Think about this for a moment.

Distribute Handout 5, "Celebrating Family Traditions."

You can use the first part of this handout as a way to jog your memory as you think about important family traditions, customs, stories, and so on. You might want to jot down some of these on the handout. In a moment I'll ask you to find a partner and share some of your family customs and traditions with your partner.

Read aloud the first part of the handout, "Traditions and Customs in Our Family," or ask a volunteer to read it. You might want to offer some examples to stimulate thinking about the various categories. Allow about a minute or so for the participants to think about the handout and make notes.

> **Every family has its own stories, games, songs, and special times that have been passed from one generation to the next.**

Now I'd like you to find a partner—someone you don't know well—and take four minutes to tell each other about some of the things you thought of in response to the handout. Make sure you allow enough time for each partner to share.

Allow time for this.

And now I'd like each pair to link up with another pair. This time I'd like each partner from the original pair to tell your group about one thing in the discussion you just had with your partner that made a special impression on you—one of your partner's family traditions, customs, or stories that stands out for you. In each group everyone will have a chance to share something about his or her partner. We'll take another four minutes for this.

Allow time for sharing within the small groups. Then bring everyone together for closure.

Closure

- *How many of you heard about a family tradition or custom that's also a tradition or custom in your own family?*
- *Who would like to share an example with the group?*
- *How many of you heard about family traditions or customs that were completely new to you?*
- *Who would like to share an example with the group?*

Ask the group to look at the second part of the handout, "Ways to Preserve Family Traditions and Customs." Read this aloud or ask a volunteer to read it.

I'd like to encourage all of you to take this handout home, share it with your families, and try some new ways to celebrate and preserve your family customs and traditions that are mentioned on the handout. Good luck and happy celebrating!

8. Summarize the meeting. (10 minutes)

Ask everyone to turn to a partner and share two thoughts or two new pieces of information he or she will take home as a result of the meeting.

Encourage participants to take the handout home, share it with their families, and try some new ways to celebrate family customs and traditions.

Closure

- *What have you enjoyed most about this meeting?*
- *What is one thing you might try as a result of this meeting?*
- *How do you think something you have learned or thought about at this meeting can strengthen self-confidence in your child?*

9. Complete the evaluation forms. (5 minutes)

Ask the group to complete the meeting evaluation form. You and others on the organizing team may wish to complete the form for meeting leaders so you can compare your reactions and plan for future meetings.

10. Provide refreshments and a social time.

Invite the group to stay for refreshments and a social time. Be sure to encourage the participants to sign up for the different roles they can take in the program. Post the sign-up sheets where they will be easy to see. Point out that even if it's late in the year, they can become involved in some of these activities next year.

Lions-Quest *Skills for Growing* at a Glance

Classroom Curriculum

▪ **Service Learning**

▪ *Together Times* **Student-Family Activity Booklets**

Positive School Climate

Parents as Partners

Community Involvement

Training and Follow-up Support

Together Times
Student-Family Activity Booklets

One per student per unit

Fun, interactive

Reinforce skills taught in the units

Reinforce skills in reading, writing, speaking, and listening

Activity sheets to be completed at school

Presented as a gift to families at the end of the unit

Treasure Hunt

Instructions: Search for people who have the interests written on the treasure hunt map. Fill in their name and specific interests.

likes sports

which ones?

_____

_____

enjoys cooking

what kinds of dishes?

_____

_____

likes to play games with kids

STAY ON TRAIL

which games?

_____

_____

collects something

TO WHOM IT MAY CONCERN

what?

_____

_____

likes to read

KONG CAVE

what book or books?

_____

_____

has a special hobby

what is it?

_____

_____

enjoys things to do as a family

what kinds of things?

_____

_____

has favorite TV shows

QUICK SAND

which ones?

_____

_____

Sources of Self-confidence

Robert Reasoner, an expert on self-esteem in children, has developed a list of key steps in the process of strengthening self-confidence based on children's needs. Parents can help to strengthen self-confidence by providing as much support as possible to meet these various needs.

Children's Needs	Adult's Role
A sense of security 	Set realistic limits Enforce rules consistently Develop self-respect and responsibility Build trust
A strong self-concept 	Provide feedback on behavior Recognize children's strengths Demonstrate love and acceptance
A sense of belonging 	Provide a supportive environment Provide children with meaningful family roles and responsibilities
A sense of purpose 	Convey expectations Provide encouragement and faith Help children set goals
A sense of personal competence 	Provide opportunities for choices and learning new skills Praise and recognize effort Help children evaluate their progress in attaining goals Provide recognition and rewards Teach children the skills they need to be successful at home

Source: Reasoner, R., *Building Self-esteem: Teacher's Guide and Classroom Materials*, Consulting Psychologists Press, Palo Alto, CA, 1982

Strengthening Self-confidence in Children

Think of at least two things you're doing or could do to strengthen self-confidence in your child for each of the following three categories:

Opportunities for my child to feel more capable in the family:

Ways to help my child feel that he or she is worthwhile, valued, and important to our family:

Ways to encourage a sense of responsibility in my child:

Travel Time, Mealtime, Bedtime

In today's busy world it's often hard for parents to find time for their children. Travel time, mealtime, and bedtime can provide precious opportunities for parents and children to interact, talk, and have fun together. Think of some things you already do or would like to do with your child for each of the following categories that will enrich your time together.

Travel Time

Mealtime

Bedtime

Celebrating Family Traditions

Families have many different ways of passing on their traditions and unique qualities. These include stories, games, recipes, memories of things family members have done, photographs, mementos and keepsakes, and many others. Think of some special traditions and customs in your family for the following categories, or add some of your own.

Traditions and Customs in Our Family

Stories:

Songs:

Special words or sayings:

Games:

Celebrations/anniversaries:

Foods/recipes:

Memories of the past:

Add some of your own categories:

Ways to Preserve Family Customs and Traditions

Try some of the following activities with your family.

• Write down special family stories or sayings and keep them in a book.

• Start a family scrapbook with mementos from special occasions, e.g., ticket stubs, menus, and so on.

• Start or update a book of photographs.

• Begin a collection of videotapes about special family occasions or celebrations.

• Make audiocassettes with family members saying what's special about the family and remembering special family stories and times together.

• Keep a file of favorite family recipes.

• Add ideas of your own.

Meeting Evaluation Form for Leaders

Meeting Three: Celebrating the Family

1. How would you rate the success of this meeting?

1	2	3	4	5
Unsuccessful				Very successful

2. What parts of the meeting were most successful?

_____

_____

3. What parts of the meeting were least successful?

_____

_____

4. What changes would you suggest in the content of the meeting?

_____

_____

5. What changes would you suggest for the meeting guide, charts, overheads, or hand-outs?

_____

_____

6. Other comments:

_____

_____

_____

Meeting Evaluation Form for Parents

Meeting Three: Celebrating the Family

We want to know what you liked and did not like about this meeting. Please let us know by filling out this page.

1. I thought the meeting was (please circle one number):

1	2	3	4	5
Not helpful				Very helpful

2. The thing I liked best about the meeting was:

_____

_____

3. I liked the way the leader:

_____

_____

4. I wish the leader had:

_____

_____

5. The next time you have this meeting think about:

_____

_____

6. I would also like to learn more about:

_____

_____

_____

Developing Your Own Parent Meetings

This guide provides you with three fully scripted parent meetings that cover many of the most important concepts and skills in the Lions-Quest *Skills for Growing* program. You may wish to cover some topics not included in these meetings, however, or develop meetings focusing on related topics. You may also want to organize meetings in subsequent program years that don't duplicate the three meetings presented in this guide. This section offers tips on how to develop successful parent meetings on your own.

You may wish to cover some topics not included in the previous meetings or develop meetings focusing on related topics.

Selecting a Topic

Your selection of topics will probably be the most important decision you make during the planning process. One way to select topics would be to send out a letter to the parents in your school listing proposed topics and requesting them to check off their preferences, perhaps in rank order, and return a response slip by a certain date. Topics might range from specific aspects of the *Skills for Growing* curriculum not covered in these meetings to broader issues, such as homework, discipline, and sibling rivalry. You might also try to determine if parents are interested in a specific type of support group, e.g., for single parents or parents of handicapped children. A sample assessment letter may be found at the end of this section.

How the Parent Meetings are Structured

We recommend that you structure each meeting, like the ones in this guide, to include a balance of presentation and interaction. The meetings begin with a "low-risk" level of involvement, giving the participants time to be-

"Neatness counted."

Be sure to allow time for interaction and closure questions.

come comfortable, and gradually progress toward more active involvement.

Since a main goal of the meetings is to encourage interaction among the participants, be sure to allow time for closure questions. The parents will appreciate this time to share their thoughts and feelings and learn about the experiences of other parents with children the same age as theirs. You may want to do this processing in large groups, small groups, or pairs.

As we've noted throughout this guide, having children participate in the meetings can be a key to parents' interest and attendance. Children can lead activities from the curriculum, perform skits, act as greeters, and hand out materials, among other roles.

A Basic Structure for Your Own Parent Meetings

1. Welcome the participants.

Plan on spending a few minutes introducing yourself and welcoming others.

2. Review the topics, goals, and agenda.

At each meeting introduce the main topic, the goals, and the activities and presentations you've planned. If you prefer to conduct an open-ended meeting, take some time to discuss which topics the parents would like to focus on.

You may want to spend a few minutes reviewing skills, concepts, and information students have been learning in *Skills for Growing* classes.

You may want to spend a few minutes reviewing the skills, concepts, and information students have been learning in their *Skills for Growing* classes. This presentation should be brief. The main message to convey is that parents are their children's first teachers and the program is designed to reinforce the positive life skills parents are teaching their children at home.

3. Complete an "icebreaker" activity.

A key part of every parent meeting is community building. Often the participants won't know each other and consequently will be hesitant about participating in discussions and sharing their thoughts and experiences with the group. To establish the necessary comfort level we recommend that you include a short "icebreaker" activity to help relax the group.

You could choose from any of the Ticklers and Energizers in the *Skills for Growing* Curriculum Guides. Also, several "icebreaker" activities are included at the end of this section.

4. Describe or review the *Skills for Growing* program.

Plan to provide a brief overview of the program's goals, components, materials, and ways of linking the home, school, and community. For the first meeting of the year, this overview might be fairly detailed. For subsequent meetings, a brief overview will suffice. You may wish to hand out the *Skills for Growing* overview from Parent Meeting One and encourage the group to read it on their own. This will be especially appropriate if most of the participants attended previous meetings.

5. Introduce an activity from the curriculum.

A key goal of the parent meetings is to offer parents hands-on experience with some of the *Skills for Growing* classroom activities. We suggest that you plan to present one of the program's key concepts or skills by involving parents in an activity similar to what their children have experienced in class. It's okay to use an activity developed for children—don't feel you have to rewrite the lesson to make it appropriate for adults. Remember, one reason the parents have come to the meeting is to find out what their children are learning in class.

It would be especially appropriate to use a lesson from the curriculum "as is" if children are part of the group, and many schools choose to involve students at this point. Children may teach parts of a lesson (depending on the grade level) or demonstrate skills through skits and other presentations. They may also prepare a display of their artwork and class assignments. Presenting les-

A short "icebreaker" helps to establish the necessary comfort level.

You don't need to rewrite the lesson for adults.

son content through actual student involvement is one of the best ways to keep parents involved and interested.

> We recommend that the children not participate in the second half of the meeting. This gives the adults an opportunity to talk among themselves. You'll need to provide separate activities for the children, such as a video or games, for the time they are not part of the meeting. An adult or older student should be assigned to supervise.

"I can't understand it. He used to be such a good egg."

6. Complete another activity from the curriculum.

Assuming you've decided not to have the children participate in the second half of the meeting, this would be a good time for an activity that will be of particular personal value and interest to the adults. Generally, the skill-building activities that focus on improving communication, cooperation, problem solving, decision making, and validation are most appropriate. This time you might want to make adjustments to the lesson so it will be more appropriate for an adult audience.

Make sure the activity is highly interactive. Experiences involving pairs and small groups are especially recommended.

7. Identify community resources.

Many parents appreciate knowing what resources the community offers to families. You can provide this information either through fliers and handouts or by asking group members to suggest five or six organizations or agencies of special value to families.

8. Summarize the meeting.

Take at least five minutes for the participants to share their impressions of the meeting. Questions might include:

- What have you enjoyed most?
- What did you find most worthwhile to you as a parent?
- What have you learned about the program you didn't know before?
- What new idea or insight will you take home from this meeting? How do you think you could apply it at home?

9. Complete the evaluation forms.

The evaluation forms included in the three parent meetings in this guide should be appropriate for your purposes. Feel free to design more specific evaluation forms if necessary.

10. Provide refreshments and a social time.

Be sure to invite the group to stay for refreshments and a social time. At each meeting encourage the participants to sign up for the different roles they can take in the program.

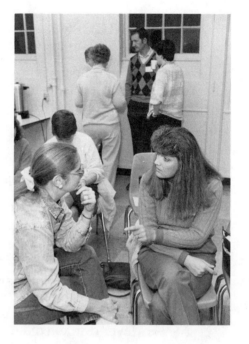

Icebreakers

People Search. Give everyone a list of questions on a sheet of paper. Ask them to stand up and move around the room meeting as many people as possible. The object is to "find someone who . . ." fills each category on the sheet and write that person's name in the space provided. Examples:

Find someone who . . .

Eats pizza

Rides a bike to work

Drives a foreign car

Was born in another city

Wears contact lenses

Has a brother or a sister

Enjoys spicy foods

Never drinks coffee

Enjoys swimming

Has at least three children

Allow about five minutes, or until all the participants have filled in their sheets as much as they can. Then ask them to call out who meets which criteria and how many categories are shared by more than one person.

Structured Introduction. Ask the participants to take turns introducing themselves to the rest of the group by using this structure:

My name is _____

I have ___ children named _____

I am here because _____

One thing I felt good about in the last couple of days was

_____

Begin by introducing yourself to set the tone. Stress that parents should say only what they feel comfortable saying and emphasize the right to pass.

Clustering. Ask the participants to stand up and move around the room meeting people as you call out the instructions. Since this will be noisy, demonstrate a signal for quiet, such as holding your hand high in the air. Ask everyone to find and get together with

- Everyone who shares the same birthday month
- Everyone who's wearing the same color shoes
- Everyone who was born within a 50-mile radius

Keep this icebreaker moving rapidly.

Who Are You? Ask the participants to jot down on a piece of paper three questions they would like to ask a person they're meeting for the first time. Encourage them to be creative with this, avoiding routine questions like "What job do you do?" Then ask them to begin moving around exchanging questions and answers and meeting as many new people as possible. After this have them sit down again and begin introducing themselves to the large group. As each person introduces himself or herself, others who have "interviewed" that person can add interesting items of information.

Introduction by Association. Explain that the participants will go around the room introducing themselves according to a specific formula. They'll begin with their names, then add some information you designate. Examples:

- A feeling
- A reason why I can't come to school today

The information they add must begin with the same letter as the person's name. For example: "My name is Sandra, and I'm feeling serious"or "My name is Mary, and I can't come to school today because I've got measles."

Name Graffiti. Ask everyone to sit in a circle. Place a large sheet of chart paper and some marker pens in the center. Beginning with yourself, ask the participants to take turns writing their names on the paper and then saying something about their name to the group. Example: "My name is Jane, and I was named after my grandmother."

Sample Assessment Letter

Dear Parents:

As part of the Lions-Quest *Skills for Growing* program at _____
School, we're planning a series of three meetings for parents that we hope
you'll find interesting and helpful.

To make sure of this, we'd like to know your opinion of several topics we're
considering for the meetings. The possible topics are:

Topic 1: _____

Topic 2: _____

Topic 3: _____

Topic 4: _____

Topic 5: _____

Topic 6: _____

Others : _____

_____

_____

Please choose the three topics you would find most important and useful.
Then return the attached response slip with your three choices in rank order.
Number "1" would be the most important and number "3" the least impor-
tant. Please return your response slip to _____ (name of person) _____

by _____ (date) _____.

Thank you.

Sincerely,

Response Slip

Here are the three meeting topics, in order of importance, that I would find most interesting:

1. _____
2. _____
3. _____

Please also consider the following topics you haven't listed:

A. _____
B. _____

Name _____

Phone number (optional) _____

Child's name _____

Teacher's name _____

Appendixes

Sample Press Release

FOR IMMEDIATE RELEASE

_____(date)_____

Contact: Name, address, phone number
of person to contact

_____(school name)_____

Adopts Nationally Acclaimed Program
To Combat Drug Use
And Related Youth Problems

Beginning _____(date program begins)_____, _____(name of school)_____ School
will offer students and parents a new program to combat drug use, alienation, and other problems of youth by helping students lead happier, healthier,
more successful lives. The program, called Lions-Quest *Skills for Growing*,
was developed by Quest International, a nonprofit educational organization
widely recognized as a world leader in creating programs for positive youth
development.

The program includes a series of meetings for parents that will be held at
_____(place where meetings will be held)_____ on _____(dates and
times of meetings)_____.

Skills for Growing is endorsed by Lions Clubs International, the National Association of Elementary School Principals (NAESP), the National PTA, and
other national organizations. According to NAESP Deputy Executive Director
Edward P. Keller, "This is one of the most ambitious projects in our
association's history. This unprecedented partnership with Quest represents
a tremendous opportunity to develop and deliver a much-needed program to
the country's more than 70,000 elementary schools."

Skills for Growing is widely recognized as the most thorough and comprehensive of numerous drug abuse prevention programs developed for elementary
schools in recent years. It offers five main components:

- A classroom curriculum for grades K-5 with lessons for an entire year
- A systematic approach to school climate improvement that will lead to numerous schoolwide activities and events
- Strong parent involvement through family-oriented projects connected with the curriculum and a series of meetings for parents where they can discuss issues of mutual concern
- Community involvement and support through volunteer efforts and projects that will enable students to work closely with people in the community
- An in-depth training workshop provided by Quest International as preparation for the program

Resources

Publications

Effective Schools and Positive School Climate

Howard, E., Howell, B., and Brainard, E. *Handbook for Conducting School Climate Improvement Projects*. Bloomington, IN: The Phi Delta Kappa Educational Foundation, 1987.

> This guide to school climate improvement is filled with useful suggestions, forms, and checklists for conducting a thorough climate assessment and improvement program.

Northwest Regional Educational Laboratory. *Effective School Practices: A Research Synthesis*. Portland, OR: Northwest Regional Educational Laboratory, April 1984.

> An excellent synthesis of hundreds of research studies on effective schools, including research on teaching, leadership, school climate, and related factors.

O'Neal, D., O'Neal, M., Short, M.L., Holmes, C.T., Brown, C.L., DeWeese, L.S., and Carter, M. *Improving School Climate*. University of Georgia Bureau of Educational Services Monographs in Education—No. 3, Spring 1987.

> A thorough review of the research on effective schools and school climate.

> Available from:

> Bureau of Educational Services
> G-9 Aderhold Hall
> College of Education
> University of Georgia
> Athens, GA 30602

Ontario Institute for Studies in Education. *Books, Tests, Kits, Journals*. Toronto: Ontario Institute for Studies in Education, 1989.

> A comprehensive catalog of resources on school improvement for teachers, school counselors, administrators, students, parents, vocational counselors, and psychologists.

Available from:

Ontario Institute for Studies in Education
OISE Press—Guidance Centre
252 Bloor St. W
Toronto, Ontario M5S 1V5
416/926-4723

U.S. Department of Education. *Reaching for Excellence: An Effective Schools Sourcebook.* Washington, DC: U.S. Department of Education, 1985.

> A collection of thoughtful essays by leading experts on a wide range of effective school studies.

Available from:

Teaching and Instruction Division
Teaching and Learning Program
National Institute of Education
Mail Stop 1805, 1200 9th St. NW
Washington, DC 20208
202/254-5407

Drug Abuse Prevention

Committees of Correspondence. *Drug Prevention Resources.* Danvers, MA: Committees of Correspondence, 1989.

> A thorough review of media and materials focusing on the prevention of alcohol and drug use for a variety of audiences.

Available from:

Committees of Correspondence
57 Conant St.
Danvers, MA 01923
508/774-2641

DuPont, R. *Getting Tough on Gateway Drugs.* Washington, DC: American Psychiatric Press, 1984.

> Straight talk on the problems associated with alcohol and other drug use among youth—and how to prevent youthful drug use.

Government of Canada. *Action on Drug Abuse: Making a Difference.* Ottawa: Minister of Supply and Services Canada, 1988.

> A report on Canadian Government activities to address the problem of alcohol and other drug use.

Johnston, L., Bachman, J., and O'Malley, P. *National Trends in Drug Use and Related Factors Among American High School Students and Young Adults, 1975-1986.* Washington, DC: U.S. Government Printing Office, 1987.

> A review of data from the most comprehensive survey available on youthful drug use and attitudes toward drugs.

Statistics Canada. *Canadian Social Trends.* Ottawa: Statistics Canada, 1989.

> This quarterly publication offers a complete picture of a variety of trends, including those affecting youth, families, and drug use.

> Available from:

> Publication Sales
> Statistics Canada
> Ottawa, Ontario K1A OT6
> 800/267-6677

U.S. Department of Education. *What Works: Schools Without Drugs.* Washington, DC: U.S. Government Printing Office, 1986.

> A review of information about school-based programs aimed at the prevention of alcohol and other drug problems.

U.S. Department of Education. *Drug Prevention Curricula: A Guide to Selection and Implementation.* Washington, DC: U.S. Government Printing Office, 1988.

> Developed by a committee of experts on drug education and prevention, this booklet offers an up-to-date overview of approaches and guidelines for effective prevention programming.

Organizations

Canada

Addiction Research Foundation

33 Russell St.
Toronto, Ontario M5S 2S1
416/595-6000 or toll-free (in Canada only) 800/387-2916

An agency of the Province of Ontario that operates specialized research, educational, clinical, and community-service programs. Write or phone for a catalog of literature and audiovisual materials.

Alberta Alcohol and Drug Abuse Commission

10909 Jasper Ave.
Edmonton, Alberta T5J 3M9
403/427-7319

Provides information and programs from a health promotion perspective related to the prevention and treatment of alcohol and drug abuse. Specific programs are available for young people.

Alcohol and Drug Concerns, Inc.

11 Progress Ave., Suite 200
Scarborough, Ontario M1P 4S7
416/293-3400

A nonprofit educational organization that sponsors conferences for young people and training in addiction issues for professionals.

Canadian Home and School and Parent-Teacher Federation

323 Chapel St.
Ottawa, Ontario K1N 7Z2
613/234-7292

Promotes public education programs on drug use and abuse and has identified smoking prevention as a priority.

Council on Drug Abuse

698 Weston Rd., Suite 17
Toronto, Ontario M6N 3R3
416/763-1491

A nonprofit organization that co-sponsors alcohol and other drug education programs for students, teachers, and parents.

Drug Enforcement Directorate

Royal Canadian Mounted Police
1200 Vanier Pkwy.
Ottawa, Ontario K1A 0R2

Provides information on drug abuse and develops cooperative working relationships with schools and communities for drug abuse prevention.

Health Promotion Directorate

Health and Welfare Canada
Fourth Floor, Jeanne Mance Bldg.
Ottawa, Ontario K1A 1B4

Provides information on health programs, many of which relate to children and youth. Also publishes a quarterly booklet on health topics and a directory of health-related organizations in Canada.

Lions Clubs

Lions Clubs International is a major co-sponsor of the *Skills for Growing* program. Contact your local Club to discuss ways for members to be involved.

Parents Against Drugs

70 Maxome Ave.
Willowdale, Ontario M2M 3K1
416/225-6604

Offers a network of services in Canada: support groups led by trained parents, a peer counseling program, a crisis telephone line for parents, public forums and presentations, and a drug awareness workshop for educators and police officers.

Parents' Resource Institute for Drug Education, Inc. (PRIDE)

PRIDE Canada
Suite 111, Thorvaldson Bldg.
College of Pharmacy
University of Saskatchewan
Saskatoon, Saskatchewan S7N 0W0
800/667-3747

Aims at increasing public awareness of alcohol and other drug problems and offers extensive resources for parents and teachers, including national conferences and research studies, a newsletter, speakers, training, and a toll-free information line.

United States

American Association of School Administrators

1801 N. Moore St.
Arlington, VA 22209
703/528-0700

AASA has a long-standing commitment to parent involvement in the schools. The booklet *Parents . . . Partners in Education* is available for bulk purchase. Also offers a video program in Spanish, *Los Padres . . . Participantes in Educacion.*

Drug-Free Schools Recognition Program

Room 508, CP
555 New Jersey Ave., NW
Washington, DC 20208-5645
202/357-6155

A competitive evaluation and award program to identify and recognize elementary and secondary schools implementing comprehensive prevention programs that have succeeded in reducing student substance abuse. Sponsored by the U.S. Department of Education.

Families in Action

3845 No. Druid Hills Rd., Suite 300
Decatur, GA 30033

Publishes a newsletter on drug information and prevention and operates a drug information center.

Focus on the Family

> 50 East Foothill Blvd.
> Arcadia, CA 91006
> 818/445-0495

> Provides references to Christian counselors and parents and publishes *Focus on the Family*, a monthly magazine.

Home and School Institute, Inc.

> Special Projects Office
> 1201 16th St., NW
> Washington, DC 20036

> Conducts demonstration projects, training programs, and conferences designed to integrate the resources of the home, school, and community. Publishes a variety of educational materials with a special emphasis on "home-style" learning for use by working parents and single parents.

Just Say No International

> 1777 No. California Blvd.
> Walnut Creek, CA 94596
> 415/939-6666 or (outside California) 800/CLUBS NO

> The leading organization in the country that supports Just Say No clubs. Provides newsletters, manuals for starting clubs, materials for club members, and other information.

Lions Clubs

> Lions Clubs International is a major co-sponsor of the *Skills for Growing* program. Contact your local Club to discuss ways for members to be involved.

National Association of Elementary School Principals

> 1615 Duke St.
> Alexandria, VA 22314-3483
> 703/684-3345

> Also a co-sponsor of *Skills for Growing*, NAESP is a national leadership organization in the field of elementary education. NAESP offers a wide variety of publications, state-level activities, and conferences every year.

National Clearinghouse for Alcohol and Drug Information

> P.O. Box 2345
> Rockville, MD 20852
> 301/468-2600

> Provides a wide variety of publications and information related to the prevention of alcohol and other drug problems, including an extensive list of publications from the National Institute on Drug Abuse, the National Institute on Alcohol Abuse and Alcoholism, and the Office for Substance Abuse Prevention.

National Committee for Citizens in Education

> 410 Wilde Lake Village Green
> Columbia, MD 21044
> 301/997-9300

> To help parents and citizens become involved in education decisions at the local level NCCE offers a toll-free hotline (800/NETWORK), a series of jargon-free handbooks and films, a training program, a computerized education clearinghouse for parents, and school-based management training to help parents and educators work together constructively.

National Council of La Raza

> 20 F St., NW
> Washington, DC 20001
> 202/628-9600

> Provides technical assistance and materials on Hispanic education issues, including parent involvement in schools. Has also developed five curriculum models that involve community-based education.

National Federation of Parents for Drug-Free Youth

> 1423 No. Jefferson
> Springfield, MO 65802-1988
> 417/836-3709

> Offers information on preventing drug and alcohol use, influences legislation, and acts as a clearinghouse for printed material and media. Also supports a team training program called "REACH, America" and a junior high school training program called "LIFERS."

National Forum of Catholic Parent Organizations

> National Catholic Education Association
> 1077 30th St., NW, Suite 100
> Washington, DC 20007

> Fosters the formation of parent groups and encourages parent participation in education. Provides a quarterly publication, *The Catholic Parent*, and offers materials to enhance parent involvement in Catholic schools.

National PTA

> 700 No. Rush St.
> Chicago, IL 60611-2571
> 312/787-0977

> The third major co-sponsor of *Skills for Growing*, the National PTA has 6.6 million members and offers leadership, information, and publications in three major areas: support on behalf of children and youth before governmental agencies and other organizations that make decisions affecting children; assistance to parents in developing the skills they need to raise and protect their children; and encouragement of parent and public involvement in the public schools.

Parents' Resource Institute for Drug Education, Inc. (PRIDE)

> PRIDE, Inc.
> 100 Edgewood Ave.
> Atlanta, GA 30303
> 800/241-7946

> Aims to increase public awareness of alcohol and other drug problems and offers extensive resources for parents and teachers, including national conferences and research studies, a newsletter, speakers, training, and a toll-free information line.

U.S. Department of Education

Regional Centers for Drug-Free Schools and Communities

> Five regional centers have been designated by the Department of Education to provide resources for training and technical assistance to state agencies, schools, and communities. Contact the center in your region for further information.

Northeast Regional Center

Super Teams, Ltd.
12 Overton Ave.
Sayville, NY 11782
516/589-7022

Connecticut, Delaware, Maine, Maryland, Massachusetts, New Hampshire, New Jersey, New York, Ohio, Pennsylvania, Rhode Island, Vermont

Southeast Regional Center

PRIDE, Inc.
100 Edgewood Ave.
Atlanta, GA 30303
404/688-9227

Alabama, District of Columbia, Florida, Georgia, Kentucky, North Carolina, Puerto Rico, South Carolina, Tennessee, Virginia, Virgin Islands, West Virginia

Midwest Regional Center

BRASS Foundation
2001 No. Clybourn Ave., Suite 302
Chicago, IL 60614
312/883-8888

Indiana, Illinois, Iowa, Michigan, Minnesota, Missouri, Nebraska, North Dakota, South Dakota, Wisconsin

Southwest Regional Center

University of Oklahoma
555 Constitution Ave.
Norman, OK 73037
405/325-1711

Arizona, Arkansas, Colorado, Kansas, Louisiana, Mississippi, New Mexico, Oklahoma, Texas, Utah

Western Regional Center

Northwest Regional Education Laboratory
101 SW Main St., Suite 500
Portland, OR 97204
503/275-9479

Alaska, American Samoa, California, Guam, Hawaii, Idaho, Montana, Nevada, Northern Marianas, Oregon, Trust Territory of the Pacific Islands, Washington, Wyoming

Bibliography

Benard, B. 1987. "Knowing what to do—and not to do—reinvigorates drug education." *ASCD Curriculum Update*, February.

Botvin, G. 1984. Drug abuse and drug abuse research. *The First Triennial Report to Congress from the Secretary, Dept. of Health and Human Services.* Washington, DC: Dept. of Health and Human Services.

Bronfenbrenner, U. 1986. Alienation and the four worlds of childhood. *Phi Delta Kappan*, February.

Canadian Youth Foundation. 1988. *Canada's Youth: "Ready for Today."* Ottawa: Canadian Youth Foundation.

DuPont, R. 1984. *Getting Tough on Gateway Drugs.* Washington, DC: American Psychiatric Press.

Glenn, H.S. and Nelsen, J. 1987. *Raising Children for Success.* Fair Oaks, CA: Sunrise Press.

Goodlad, J. 1984. *A Place Called School.* New York: McGraw-Hill.

Gordon, I. 1979. The effects of parent involvement on schooling. In *Partners: Parents and Schools.* Alexandria, VA: Association for Supervision and Curriculum Development.

Hawkins, J.D., Lishner, D.M., Catalano, R.F., Jr., and Howard, M.O. 1986. Childhood predictors of adolescent substance abuse: Toward an empirically grounded theory. *Journal of Children in Contemporary Society*, 18 (12):11-48.

Hodgkinson, H. 1985. *All One System.* Washington, DC: Institute for Educational Leadership.

Johnston, L., Bachman, J., and O'Malley, P. 1987. *National Trends in Drug Use and Related Factors Among American High School Students and Young Adults, 1975-1986.* Washington, DC: U.S. Government Printing Office.

Lezotte, L. 1985. Speech presented to the Administrative Council, Waterford, Michigan, October 1985.

PRIDE, Canada, Inc. and Drug Enforcement Directorate, Royal Canadian Mounted Police. 1987. *Youth and Drugs: What Parent Groups Can Do to Create Drug Resistant Communities.* Ottawa: Royal Canadian Mounted Police.

Saskatchewan Alcohol and Drug Abuse Commission. 1986. *Alcohol, Drugs, and Youth.* Regina, Saskatchewan: Saskatchewan Alcohol and Drug Abuse Commission.

Selman, R.O. 1980. *The Growth of Interpersonal Understanding.* New York: Academic Press.

Sizer, T. 1985. *Horace's Compromise.* Boston: Houghton Mifflin.

Statistics Canada. 1986. *Dwellings and Households.* Ottawa: Statistics Canada.

U.S. Department of Education. 1986a. *Schools Without Drugs.* Washington, DC: U.S. Government Printing Office.

_____. 1986b. *What Works: Research About Teaching and Learning.* Washington, DC: U.S. Government Printing Office.

_____. 1988. *Drug Prevention Curricula: A Guide to Selection and Implementation.* Washington, DC: U.S. Government Printing Office.

Acknowledgments

The following schools have played an important role in the development of Lions-Quest *Skills for Growing*. Their "hands-on" experience with the materials and their wisdom about the needs of children, schools, families, and communities have significantly shaped and refined the program.

Canadian Pilot Schools

Aldergrove Elementary School
Margaret-Ann Young, Principal
Edmonton, Alberta

Dunluce Community School
Keith Middleton, Principal
Edmonton, Alberta

Langley Meadows Elementary School
Walter Krahn, Principal
Langley, British Columbia

Riverview Public School
James Ferguson, Principal
Cumberland, Ontario

United States Pilot Schools

Aboite Elementary School
John E. Flora, Principal
Fort Wayne, IN

Bridgeport Elementary School
Joey Duncan, Principal
Bridgeport, TX

Brush College Elementary School
David R. King, Principal
Salem, OR

Cape Cod Academy
Sue Leary, Administrator
Osterville, MA

Cleveland Elementary School
Ardeth Hearn, Principal
Lawton, OK

Coolidge Elementary School
William Brousard, Principal
Cedar Rapids, IA

Effie Green Elementary School
James W. McCall, Principal
Raleigh, NC

Epperly Heights Elementary School
James D. Johnson, Principal
Del City, OK

Fairmoor Elementary School
Lynne Wake, Principal
Columbus, OH

W. H. Fuller GT Magnet Elementary School
Peggy J. Beasley-Rodgers, Principal
Raleigh, NC

Ganado Intermediate School
William Soder, Principal
Ganado, AZ

Ganado Primary School
Sigmond Boloz, Principal
Dr. Ronald Brutz, Director of Curriculum
Ganado, AZ

Glencoe Middle School
Richard Wickmann, Principal
Julie Warweg, Chemical Health
Facilitator
Glencoe, MN

Greenbrier Elementary School
Linda Scott, Principal
Chesapeake, VA

Harbour View School
Marilyn Koeller, Principal
Huntington Beach, CA

Hazelwood Elementary School
Roger Abshire, Principal
Newark, OH

Horace Cureton Elementary School
Anita Canul, Principal
San Jose, CA

Johnson Elementary School
Cynthia Monroe, Principal
Carol Lensing, Program Facilitator
Cedar Rapids, IA

Kempton Street School
Ron Begley, Principal
Spring Valley, CA

Latimer School
Marguerite Weiner, Principal
San Jose, CA

Madison Elementary School
Sue Smith, Principal
Newark, OH

**Maryland Avenue
Demonstration School**
Sandra M. Pineda, Principal
La Mesa, CA

Meeteetse Consolidated Schools
Kent Cook, Principal
Meeteetse, WY

Morningside Elementary School
William Sorrell, Principal
Elizabethtown, KY

Wings Park Elementary School
Steve Bradley, Principal
Susan Dohrmann, Counselor
Oelwein, IA

Ridge Ranch School
Roger Bayersdorfer, Principal
Paramus, NJ

Park Elementary School
Fred Laborn, Principal
Janine Hooley, Drug Free Schools
Coordinator
Michigan City, IN

Dan D. Rogers Elementary School
Rex Cole, Principal
Dallas, TX

Fred A. Smith Elementary School
Gailya Winters, Principal
Richard Barfield, Assistant Principal
Raleigh, NC

St. Ann School
Mary A. Johnson, Principal
Lansing, IL

Summit Elementary School
Barbara Triplett, Principal
Summit Station, OH

Superior Elementary School
Brenda Wade, Principal
East Cleveland, OH

Tisbury Elementary School
Alan T. Campbell
Vineyard Haven, MA

Vista La Mesa School
Dan Heiserman, Principal
La Mesa, CA

Washington Elementary School
Tom L. Sipe, Principal
Gayle Young, Counselor
Ponca City, OK

North Whittier Wallen L. Andrews School
Alex Gasporra, Principal
Whittier, CA

York Elementary School
LaVerne V. Freitag, Principal
Lynn Williams English, Vice Principal
Raleigh, NC